# Eighteen Gates

Issachar Miron

# Hillel

**"Whatever is hateful unto thee, do it not unto thy fellow."**

*Hillel the Elder 30 B.C.E.–10 C.E.*

# Eighteen Gates

by

## ISSACHAR MIRON

Foreword

by

## ELIE WIESEL

Illustrations

by

## ARTHUR SZYK

From My Angle

by

## HAYIM HEFER

Epilogue

by

## RABBI IRVING GREENBERG

JASON ARONSON INC.
NORTHVALE, NEW JERSEY
LONDON

*Of Jewish Holidays and Festivals*

# Eighteen Gates

First Edition 1993

Illustrations by Arthur Szyk are reproduced by courtesy
and permission of the Arthur Szyk Estate and Family.

Music by Issachar Miron is reproduced by courtesy and permission
of the McRon Music Co., 521 Fifth Avenue, New York, NY 10017.

LIBRARY OF CONGRESS CATALOGING-IN-PUBLICATION DATA

Miron-Michrovsky, Issachar, 1920-
Eighteen gates of Jewish holidays and festivals / by Issachar Miron.
p.        cm.
ISBN 0-87668-563-7

1. Fasts and feasts--Judaism--Meditations.
2. Fasts and feasts--Judaism--Prayer-books and devotions--English.
3. Judaism--Prayer-books and devotions--English. I. Title. II. Title: 18 gates of Jewish
holidays and festivals.
BM690.M564  1993
296.4'3--dc20            92-41081

Manufactured in the Unites States of America.
JASON ARONSON INC. offers books and cassettes.
For information and catalog write to
JASON ARONSON INC.,
230 Livingston Street, Northvale, New Jersey 07647.

*To Tsipora with love*

# EIGHTEEN GATES

"Ahead of the Table of Contents"

## Gatepost Epigraph

### In Appreciation

O Father of our parents
Sarah, Rebecca, Rachel, Leah,
Miriam, Hannah, and Deborah,
Abraham, Isaac, Israel,
Joseph, Moses, Aaron, and David,
we express to You,
on every one
of the three hundred sixty-five
newborn nights and days,
our appreciation for transmitting
Your Heart's impulses
to our consciousness,
for moving Your Brain's signals
to the motherboard of our psyche,
for broadcasting
Your inter-galactic-radio-remote
wavelengths of destiny
into our internal circuits of faith
(that are to our life what
the liquid-hydrogen-oxygen propellant
is to the launching
of a space shuttle into the sky).

O Interactive Grantor
of the gift of life and learning,
restore to us:
the seeds—for love,
the wings—for hope,
the muscle—for trust,
the truth—for justice,
the harmony—for soul,
the tears—for happiness,
the equality—for freedom,
the swiftness—for compassion,
the perceptive vision—for mind,
the warmth of feeling—for heart,
the outstretched hand—for peace,
the congregational response—for Amens,
the chorale of mixed voices—for Hallelujahs,
the world full of marvels—for every day of the year,
instantly updating
our covenantal communications
as the sacred bond of equal commitment,
that's still and all emitting light of yesterday,
steeling the shield of today,
imparting the hope for tomorrow.
*Ve-im'ru: Amen.* Now respond: (Universe: Amen)

From "Wavelengths of Destiny"

*Eighteen Gates*

# Table of Contents

# Table of Contents

# Table of Contents

EIGHTEEN GATES BY ISSACHAR MIRON / TABLE OF CONTENTS / EIGHTEEN GATES

# Table of Contents

## Dancing unto the Lord

*"Let Israel rejoice in his Maker;*
*Let the children of Zion be joyful in their King.*
*Let them praise His name in the dance."*

Psalm 149:2–3

# FOREWORD

## ISSACHAR MIRON

*by*

## *Elie Wiesel*

Make prayers out of my tales, said Rabbi Nachman of Bratzlav. His followers obeyed and went even further: they made tales out of his prayers. As for his distant disciple, Franz Kafka, he simply stated: to write is to pray.

Literature and prayer have much in common. Both take everyday words and give them meaning. Both appeal to what is most personal and most transcendent in man. Both are rooted in the most obscure and mysterious zone of our being. Nourished by anguish and fervor, both negate detachment and imitation—and are negated by them.

The writer and the worshiper both draw from one source—the source where sound becomes melody, and melody turns into language which becomes offering. What inspiration is to the writer, *kavvanah* is to the beseecher. Both are as open as an open wound—both live tense and privileged moments.

If one may assume that man could not live without literature, one may equally affirm that neither could he survive without prayer. Except that in our society it is becoming increasingly difficult for modern man to pray: He has conquered space but forgotten his prayer.

This is particularly true of our young people. Some of us remember their outburst of emotion when they reached the Western Wall in 1967. Many did not know what to do, what to say. I remember the Simḥat Torah celebration in Moscow. Many students sang and danced since they knew nothing else—and no other way—to affirm their Jewishness. Their religious thirst was greater, and more genuine, than that of their parents. What they yearned for is not knowledge but devotion; they sought fervor more than erudition.

More and more youngsters, especially of secular background, want to be taught how to pray, in what to believe—and in whom as well. I hope they will read Issachar Miron's book. His modern prayers are prayers for modern men and women who wish to express their joy and fear in contemporary terms.

To write a Jewish prayer, one has to have a musical ear and a poetic soul. Issachar Miron has both. He is a sensitive composer. His evocative and beautiful *niggunim* have the tone and weight of a moving Jewish testimony. There are poetic alliterations in his music, and musical resonances in his poetry, brightening his personal voyage of discovery into Jewish holy days with passion, warmth, and wit.

Religious holidays and secular celebrations or commemorations, historic events and individual responses to them: Miron relates to them with tact and art. But then, why shouldn't he? His songs from and for Israel earned him a wide reputation. With this book, it will be enhanced. ■

Arthur Szyk

## The Shmoozers—When Hearts Talk

"It seems that the chair is too high for you?  Isn't it?"
"Not at all.  The table is too low."

# Flower of Your Gate

Whether
sheltered
in the crannies
beneath
the barren rocks,
or
growing free
in
the wide-open spaces,
I am
like
a lonely bird.

There,
on a telephone pole—
above the earthly
tears and laughter—
I am nourished
from
the heights,
by
the golden-wheat berries
hiding inside
the grandfatherly tousled hair
of the bearded sunshine.

In that way
I bring
to your
unconscious heart
the ordinarily
unattainable
food of love,
from beyond
the limits
of awareness.

Now scent:  Amen.
(Flowers' Congregation—Amen)

I am the sole living member of my family. In the winter of 1941– 1942, along with some 7,000 other Jews, my family endured inhuman suffering in the Kutno ghetto set up by the Nazis in the ruins of the rat-ridden sugar refinery on the outskirts of our town. This short-lived Ghetto became immediately a freezing inferno of disease, starvation, and corroding degradation. In March 1942, my family, with all the other dearly beloved Kutno martyrs, perished in Chełmno—the first death camp of the "final solution of the Jewish question" in Poland. Their holy remains were buried in the nearby Rzuwowski Forest, in ditches they had been forced to dig prior to entering the poison gas death trucks. Heroic borders frame the entire page of their martyrdom. There are no survivors to tell us their unutterable story. May their memory never be forgotten!

Galaxies have changed lanes since then. Yet, I still hear them talking about Jewish holidays as if they were talking about some dearest members of our immediate family. Almost every single night—when I dream about them—their voices are still crying out in my heart.

They have gone, but their *niggun* of *Yiddishkeit*—blazing through the darkest clouds like the sun—is still singing. It is striking new roots for our continuity, love, and unity—reawakening the vitality of Jewish experience.

For this reason, it is the intention of this book to reflect my love affair with the religious and secular dimensions of the Jewish holidays, rather than attempt to contribute something new to what has been written about so exhaustively before. It is meant to whet the appetite rather than to satiate the hunger, to entertain rather than to educate.

I strive to associate myself with the reader within the integrated frontiers of contemporary Jewishness as related to its growing, cross-fertilizing milieu, Ashkenazic, Sephardic, Yemenite, and the noble newcomer, the ancient tribe of *Beta Israel* (Jewish Ethiopian), which enriches with old-new colors the tapestry of our spiritual existence.

The holidays are portrayed here in a subjective mode. They themselves unfold—often in the first person—their *own* tales, from their *own* points of view, as I imagined in my childhood they would have done in a person-to-person conversation if they had the faculty of speech. I still listen to their hallowed voices.

The earliest encouragement for this book came some eighteen years ago from Professor Moshe Davis, founder and then head of the Institute of Contemporary Jewry at the Hebrew University of Jerusalem, who, in reply to my Ḥanukkah greeting, wrote (at that time quite unaware—as was I—of the eventual impact of his words on me): "Our heartfelt אמן [*amen*] to your wonderfully special and meaningful prayer for peace and understanding. I found it challenging—so much so that I shared it with my students."

At about the same time, the late Rabbi Avraham Soltes, the chaplain of the U.S. Military Academy of West Point, to whose librettos I composed then several oratorios, including the "Golden Gates of Joy," televised by CBS coast-to-coast with the Ray Charles Singers, shared with me the depth of his wisdom, talent, and tact, constantly challenging me to compile and publish my poems, prayers, greetings, and holiday anthems. This warm endorsement and backing had a profound influence on my work.

Years later, new impetus to go ahead with *Eighteen Gates* was given by two notes that I received from the late Boris Smolar, founder and editor-in-chief of JTA, the Jewish Telegraphic Agency, which read in part: "Your holiday pieces are rich in expression, meaningful and thought-provoking. I'll keep them among the literary gems in my archives."

These three unconnected moments of inspiration were of pivotal importance to me. They encouraged me to present my work to Elie Wiesel. Only when he wrote that my "modern prayers are prayers for modern men and women who wish to express their joy and fear in contemporary terms" did I dare to prepare my book for publication. I could not have had a more meaningful endorsement. I am, indeed, much indebted to Professor Wiesel.

Eighteen Gates owes its glorious appearance to the immortal art of a venerated master—the late Arthur Szyk. In his prodigious outpouring of miniatures, paintings, illustrations, and cartoons, he found the time and interest to paint numerous Jewish masterpieces, including the modern illumination of the 1264 Charter of Kalisz (reproductions of four of which are included in the book): Passover Haggadah, Song of Esther, Israel Independence Scroll, and the Jewish Holidays series on permanent exhibition at the Yeshiva University Museum of New York City. Special thanks are offered to his daughter, Alice Szyk Bracie, and the Arthur Szyk Estate for their support of this publication.

I think I should explain now why the title of this book is *Eighteen Gates*, admitting right from the start that I am not immune from the Jewish irresistible attraction to "18." There are eighteen holy days (*Ma'asei Torah* 34:15). Eighteen times Abraham, Isaac, and Jacob are mentioned in the Torah (*Ta'anit* 2:2). One has to wear eighteen garments on the Sabbath day (*Midrash Aseret Hadibrot*). And the list goes on and on. In fact, there are twenty-one gates in *Eighteen Gates*, including the eighteen gates dedicated to holidays, as well as three additional gates: "In Front of the Gates," "On the Threshold to the Gates," and "Beyond Time, Above the Gravitation, Across Time and Space." Whatever the correct number is, their hermeneutical "eighteen" symbolism seems to prevail again over the absoluteness of arithmetic. I hope, in this spirit, *Eighteen Gates* will offer the reader some glimpses of our holidays and festivals—the unfathomable lights of our heritage—that still illuminate our lives, guiding us along their pathways and linking the disparate, personal, and universal glades of heart in the contemporary forests of faith.

Relating to the need for modern motivational material to aid the self-rejuvenating process of Jewish continuity today, within the perception of the two biblical worlds—the heavenly and the earthly—both inseparably intertwined, I invite the attention of the reader to the fact that *Eighteen Gates* embraces in its midst five present-day festivals: Yom ha-Sho'ah, Yom ha-Atzma'ut, Yom Yerushalayim, Jewish Solidarity Day, and Today and Every Day (an every-day-without-fail holiday).

In deepest gratitude I express my thanks to Ruth and the late Leon L. Gildesgame, and their sons Daniel and Myron, whose friendship has touched me and my family's life in countless ways. It was they who urged me unrelentingly to offer my writings for publication. It was difficult to resist their loving support, especially that of the then nonagenarian Leon, whom I adored and with whom I shared songs, laughter, and tears for so many years.

My warm thanks go to Hayim Hefer, a recipient of the Israel Prize for Poetry, for his personal reflections, "From My Angle"; and to the distinguished rabbi and teacher Irving Greenberg, the president of CLAL—the National Jewish Center for Learning and Leadership, who contributed the Epilogue.

I was indeed fortunate to exchange ideas with Kenny Karen, a singer, composer, and lyricist, who read the entire book several times, once even aloud for the fluidity of the verse; with Alan Marbé of Tel Aviv University; with Irving Bernstein, formerly executive vice-president of the UJA; with Marc Tabatchnik, a veteran official of the JDC and UJA; with Melvyn H. Bloom, executive vice-president of the American Friends of the Technion Society; with Paul Jeser, JNF national campaign director; with musicologist and radio and TV commentator Martin Bookspan; with Melvyn Ginsberg, an insightful reader; and with Bel Kaufman, a distinguished author and the granddaughter of Shalom Aleichem—all of whom read selected sections or the whole manuscript and offered valuable suggestions and much inspiration. I would be remiss if I did not express my gratitude to Muriel Jorgensen, the director of editorial production of Jason Aronson Inc., who displayed unique sensitivity to the creative process, as she herself perceptively observed: "One doesn't tell the artist what colors to put on the canvas"; and yet, her insightful erudition and savoir-faire were of great help, and are indeed warmly appreciated.

I offer my thanks to Professor Abraham Katsh, president of the Jewish Academy of the Arts and Sciences; to the late Oscar Schisgall, who wrote an article about my musical work in the *Readers Digest*; to the late Tuli Sonneborn and Rudolf G. Sonneborn, a towering American Jewish leader; to Robert Sherman, WQXR's executive producer of *The Listening Room*, who read some of my holiday poems in his broadcasts of my music; to Maria and Samuel H. Miller; and to Clara Louise and Henry Sonneborn III—each of whom helped in some stimulating way. As a matter of fate, *Eighteen Gates* owes its genesis to my personal holiday greetings, shared for some eighteen years with my family and close friends. In turn, it was they who urged me to publish my work, stressing the need for motivational material to project in contemporary terms the bond of Jewish continuity today within the perception of the two biblical worlds—the heavenly and the earthly, the absolute and the relative—both inseparably intertwined.

None of what has been said here should imply, in any way, that those who assisted me so thoughtfully share my views, or hold any responsibility for errors—which, if any, are *solely* my own.

The cover page calligraphy is by Tania Aleshin and some of the computer graphics by Edna Maayani. Alan C. Freed typeset the first version of this book, and then acquainted me with *PageMaker*, a desktop publishing program, enabling me to do on my own the numerous subsequent rewrites (on Macintosh IIfx), including this version for publication. Alan continued thereafter to assist me sporadically, reading some of the poems aloud, and offering friendly attention to every detail. The layout was inspired by the imaginative design (even by today's standards) of the 1482 Lisbon Hebrew Bible.

In retrospect, the love, enthusiasm, and heart-and-soul advice—and, no less important, patience—of my daughters and sons-in-law, Ruth and Michael Schleider, Shlomit and Steven Sholem, Miriam and Chet Lipton, and our six grandchildren, Jennifer, Jeffrey, Scott, Julie, Zachary, and Gabrielle, heartened me immeasurably.

Last but not least, I must now give credit where credit is most due—to my beloved wife, Tsipora Miron, my dearest friend, a consummate musicologist, pianist, and organist, who has been both my severest critic and my most exultant fan, the one who has given me wings to soar to the heavens, and yet has kept me firmly grounded on the earth. With love I dedicate this book to her.

*Issachar Miron*

_Arthur Szyk_

# Ḥad Gadya: "An only kid, an only kid!"

**The kid is Israel; the other figures, its oppressors.
The Passover parable sings of the futility of power
versus the mightiness of spirit.**

# In Front of the Gates:
# Lamps and Legends Turning On Your Headlights

*The symbolism and energy of the life-giving light is paramount in Jewish thought. The first of the divine commandments of Creation is: "Let there be light!" dispelling the darkness of the day and guiding us in each generation through the perplexities of the night.*

The old will be rejuvenated, the new will be consecrated; old and new together will be torches of light over Zion.

*Avraham Isaac Hacohen Kook (1865–1935)*
Zionism in Transition
*(The Institute of Contemporary Jewry, The Hebrew University of Jerusalem)*

I believe in the sun even when it is not shining. I believe in love even when not feeling it. I believe in God even when He is silent.

*Inscription found on a wall of a cellar in Cologne, where Jews hid from the Nazis*

And God smiled; for before He shaped man He knew the fear with which darkness would fill his heart; He knew the frustration that would burst from the inertness of his clay. And God said: Let there be light!

*Libretto and Lyrics: Avraham Soltes (1917–1983)*
*Music: Issachar Miron (1920–)*
Golden Gates of Joy Oratorio *(Warner/Chappell Music Inc.)*

In the beginning was the idea, which led to action. Now, action has to lead to the rejuvenation of the idea. Zionism stemmed from, and was motivated in the Diaspora; today the source of Zionism's power must come from the State itself.

*Moshe Davis (1916–)*

*(The Institute of Contemporary Jewry, The Hebrew University of Jerusalem)*

For the modern Jew will not indefinitely adhere to Judaism because of its antiquity, but will do so because it contains valuable ideas to which he can subscribe. A commitment of this kind is not a unique act of judgment made at a particular time but a never-ending process.

*Nathan Rotenstreich (1914–)*, Tradition and Reality
*(Random House, New York, 1972)*

## EIGHTEEN GATES OF JEWISH HOLIDAYS AND FESTIVALS

# EIGHTEEN GATES

"In Front of the Gates"

## Gatepost Epigraph

### "Smile!"

"He who makes peace
in His heights,
may He make peace upon us
and upon all Israel,"
guiding our steps.

Though
we know
this doesn't happen
overnight,
we pray every day,
sun, storm, or snow:
May
our Father, our King,
in an affirmation
of Himself,
for His
"own sake have mercy on us"
and guard His handiwork:
ourselves—against self-hatred,
humanity—against self-disintegration,
and the universe—against self-destruction.

It's going to be all right!
(Smile!)
So be it.

From "In Bonded Blue and White Bloom"

Where flowers are,
their colors kiss each other,
saturating
the air you breathe with love,
helping you stay cool
on your stormbound way.

Where flowers are,
their sense of self
prays silently for the withered,
soothing the restless,
mesmerizing the sun to shine,
spellbinding the moon
to sing with the stars.

Where flowers are,
their scent rises higher
in your soul
than the tallest trees,
dwarfing the highest hills,
daring the crops
to embrace the weeds.

Where flowers are,
their blossom-beauty reconciles
the poles of earth and sky,
forging justice,
feeling friendship,
flinging hate from our garden.

Like flowers,
our festivals reflect on earth
the savory splendor
from the scriptural gardens,
renewing your plain-spoken
commitment
to others as to yourself.

Then inhale just a tiny,
yet-larger-than-life,
puff of their redolent sanctity,
making peace with yourself,
keeping in your heart
the promise of our unity,
asking yourself:
"Isn't this what I must do
every day?"
and following your answer right away
by an even more important question:
"Have I done enough today?"

*"The time of singing is come."*

XXVII

# *Heavenly Microchips*

At
    this perilous
    moment of time
    we whisper our supplication
    with the gentle murmur of leaves
    tiptoeing together
        in the evening breezes.

We soul-express to You
    on wings of our silent meditation
    this thank-You note,
    remembering—
    at these crossroads
    of self-doubt—
    Your aiding us
    in our human fallibility,
    forging us
    by inhuman tragedy,
    sustaining us
    by superhuman hope,
    and molding within us
    an old-new Jewish consciousness.

Mindful
    of the miracles
    that caused in our day
    the unification of Jerusalem—
    the greatest light-gathering power
    in the solar system—
    planted amid
    the bare Judean hills
    and gracing the rebirth of Israel
    as its golden glory,
    we harmonize with You
    an earth-to-heaven holographic song
    harnessing our spirituality
        from each angle.

On
    every level,
    in three dimensions—
    in thought,
    in tendency
    and in tone—
    we download at lightning speed
    Your Word-processing software
    into the computer-driven program
    of our mind
    to upgrade and decode
    the tenets
    of Your Heavenly Microchips.
        Hallelujah.

# In Bonded Blue and White Bloom

For
teaching us
to stand ten feet tall,
ready to defend ourselves
body and soul against any enemy
and not to despair
even when our eyes are blindfolded,
our backs to the wall
with our hands chained behind us,
we send up to You
the rising flowers of our heart—
now breaking out efflorescent
in bonded blue and white bloom.

Beyond
conventional reasonings
we offer You
the fruits from our tree of reflectiveness
growing improbably
on a cliff's treacherous edge
hanging over a subconscious volcano—
and ask You
to grant us the strength of courage
to cling to each other
in our great solidarity
of pain and promise.

We beseech You
to enlighten us just for a while
with a tiny ray
of Jeremiah's sparkling light—
to seek You and to find You.

"He who makes peace
in His heights,
may He make peace upon us
and upon all Israel," guiding our steps.

Though
we know
this doesn't happen overnight,
we pray every day,
sun, storm, or snow:
May
our Father, our King,
in an affirmation of Himself,
for His
"own sake have mercy on us"
and guard His handiwork:
ourselves—against self-hatred,
humanity—against self-disintegration,
and the universe—against self-destruction.
It's going to be all right!  (Smile!)
So be it.

# *Wavelengths of Destiny*

Struck
    by the beauty of the new day,
  we drill Heaven's floors,
peering through each layer
    of the complexities of being
      and the poisonous pastures of complacency,
        to see the grand vistas of morality in Your Law.

We knit the dynamics of each sunrise
    with the scenic splendors of each sunset,
  marveling at the might of Your creation—
whether it be the sun,
    or the distant puff of an unexplored star,
     a mountain, or a molehill—
       all founded on truth and tolerance for all.

O Father
    of our parents
   Sarah, Rebecca, Rachel, Leah,
 Miriam, Hannah, and Deborah,
   Abraham, Isaac, Israel,
    Joseph, Moses, Aaron, and David
    we express to You,
     on every one
       of the three hundred sixty-five newborn nights,
     our appreciation for transmitting
   Your Heart's impulses to our consciousness,
  for moving Your Brain's signals
    to the motherboard of our psyche,
     for broadcasting
    Your inter-galactic-radio-remote
   wavelengths of destiny
into our internal circuits of faith
  (that are to our life
    what the liquid-hydrogen-oxygen propellant
   is to the launching
    of a space shuttle high into the sky).

O Interactive Grantor of the gift of life and learning,
    restore to us:  the seeds—for love,
  the wings—for hope,
the muscle—for trust,
  the truth—for justice,
   the harmony —for soul,
    the tears—for happiness,
     the equality—for freedom,
    the swiftness—for compassion,
   the perceptive vision—for mind,
  the warmth of feeling—for heart,
the outstretched hand—for peace,
  the congregational response—for Amens,
  the chorale of mixed voices—for Hallelujahs,
   the world full of marvels—for every day of the year,
    instantly updating our covenantal communications
   as the sacred bond of equal commitment,
that's still and all emitting the light of yesterday,
  steeling the shield for today,
   imparting the hope for tomorrow.
    *Ve-im'ru: Amen.* Now respond: (Universe: Amen)

# On the Threshold to the Gates

Jewish tradition draws its inspiration from the experiences of ordinary people. Every day is a threshold into the future. Each new dawn opens a new gate of life. Each sunset forges anew the present-day bond with the past-day inheritance. Each sunrise brings us light reflecting our attitudes to our families and communities. Day by day we add a new meaning to history. Invincibly—hour by hour—we deepen with pride our understanding of our covenantal rights. Night and day we forge our obligations vis-à-vis the fragile human worlds of faith.

We make what we can of our condition with the means available. We must accept the mixture as we find it—the impurity of it, the tragedy of it, the hope of it.

*Saul Bellow (1915–)*, Great Jewish Stories
*(Dell Publication Co., Inc., New York, 1963)*

We believe that our survival is an index of the supremacy of spiritual over material value. We believe in all humility and thanks to a merciful Providence that it has a relevance to the broad experience of mankind today.

*Yaacov Herzog (1921–1972)*, A People that Dwells Alone
*(Weidenfeld and Nicolson, London, 1975)*

Is it at all possible for a Jew not to be a Zionist? After all, the Almighty Himself "chose Zion" and is thus a Zionist; and we are commanded to emulate God and walk in His ways.

*Avraham Isaac Hakohen Kook (1865–1935)*
*Chief Rabbi of Eretz Yisrael*
*(Norman Lamm [1927–]*, Rav Kook—Man of Faith and Vision
*[Jewish National Fund, New York, 1965])*

"It must be a long time since you've prayed," a young man observed.
"Very long."
"Well, it is never too late."

*Isaac Bashevis Singer (1904–)*, The Magician of Lublin
*(Fawcett Crest Book, New York, 1980)*

EIGHTEEN GATES OF JEWISH HOLIDAYS AND FESTIVALS

# EIGHTEEN GATES

Eighteen Gates by Issachar Miron / On the Threshold to the Gates / Lord's Life-Giving Gates

Eighteen Gates by Issachar Miron / On the Threshold to the Gates / Lord's Life-Giving Gates

"On the Threshold to the Gates"

## Gatepost Epigraph

### Lord's Life-Giving Gates

I believe that
faith can illuminate
the past
for the memory of it,
rouse the present
to action
for the survival of it,
lengthen the horizons
of the future
for the promise of it,
grow a tree
for the shade of it,
nurture our trust
in others for the joy of it.

And, I believe that
together we can
nourish freedom
for the taste of it,
nurse friendship
for the touch of it,
and embrace the universe
for the peace of it.

Never letting spiritual bygones
be bygones,
we can conjure hopeful tomorrows
out of yesterday's pain,
affirming faith with faith.

Where there's a dream
there is a song
to awaken the voice,
a melody to restore the will,
and a flame
to illuminate the way.

So I believe that jointly
we can open
the Lord's life-giving gates,
turning the divine streams
of light and love
onto the salvation-thirsty
deserts of our being.

May this be our goal  now and ever after.

From "His Gardeners"

We thank You
    for commanding
    Your human-to-human spirituality
    to flow
    from Your earthly satellite,
    from us—
    the global-communications' scapegoats
    for every conceivable misfortune—
    throughout
    our all-consuming tragic,
    tormenting,
        yet miraculous voyage.

And
    we thank You
    for bringing forth
    upon us in each generation
    the long-term logic of an afterthought,
    the strength-training ripeness
    of physical renewal,
    and the alluring independence
    of a self-confident soul—
    among the descendants
        of Job and David.

Thus hiking
    into the high-hidden country
    sprawling across
    the eyewitness-telescopic meadows,
    we place on the wings
    of our silent meditation
    this picture-phone thank-You call—
    face-to-face—eye-to-eye—ear-to-ear—
    for consecrating
    and culling the Hebrew language
    from the world's 3,000 tongues
        as the holy vernacular of Your Book.

And we express every day
    our gratitude to You for picking
    from nature's resplendent
    floral displays those among the earth's palest,
    tiniest and scarcest of all roses
    and lovingly adopting us
    as Your chosen children
    endowed with the conscious day-to-day penchant
    for messianic moralities in heart and in flesh,
        within our mind, at home, and in the universe.

Hallelujah.

# *Sabra's Thorns of Love*

Think of that:
no matter how sharp-edged
and menacing
they may seem to you,
don't fear the Sabra's
prickly-pear points
and its threatening
spiny cactus needles.

For if you look a little closer,
you'll see that they're
the hardy thorns of love,
emotionally and physically,
a model of a meadow-green resilience,
a legacy of grace to follow
within and from the perspectives
of your reborn dreams.

In fact,
their resurgent,
spike-like-barbed-wire attire,
stiffly bristling
with the perplexities
of visions and reality,
is just a tranquil, yet . . .
a tough-looking self-defense conundrum
guarding the peaceful riches
of a tender soul
within a sturdy body.

Look rather at the Sabra's
motherly nest—cozy,
morally conscious—with the young,
arm-to-arm, growing heads-high,
in succulent brotherhood,
beseeching in unison the Lord's grace
for the lonely, for the disunited,
for the dispersed and deserted,
for the oppressed in great fright.

Last but dearest of all:
go and see for yourself,
how we ourselves can blossom,
breathe and bask
in the cardiopulmonary-resuscitating light
of unity,
peace and freedom,
giving thanks to the Merciful
for having brought us closer—one to another,
stronger today
and freer than yesterday.

# *Friendship*

"Well?"
    Well, only when you're strong,
    yet crying
    for every one of the tiniest
    among the billions
    of fallen stars,
    can you make friends
    with
    the mightiest of the cosmos,
    standing
    with the sun
    on equal footing
        and matchmaking the earth with the sky.

"Only?"
    Only when wearing
    your amiability
    on your sleeve,
    can you strike
    the balance between
    the protective musts
    of the husk
    and the quest
    for love of the kernel,
    reconciling
    the misinterpreted wheat
        with its misunderstood chaff.

"Only then?"
    Yes, only when walking
    through the narrow alleys
    of danger and dismay,
    can you tend
    your serenity of spirit
    on a first-name basis
    . . . and reecho the passion
    for one great
    prophetic brotherhood,
        larger than any of your cravings.

"Wherefrom?"
    From the fraternal high points
    shielded
    in your collective consciousness
    you'll see farther
    than the eye can foresee,
    feel deeper
    than the heart can forefeel,
    knowing
    that you're on good terms
        with yourself and the world.

Give then
      all the goodwill you can
      to amicability
      and you'll be able
      to perceive why
      it's the most generous
      of all gifts,
      the most endearing
        of divine blessings.

You'll see it
      jogging with you—
      hand in hand—
      accepting
      you as you are,
      comforting you
      in your grief,
      rejoicing
      with you in your success,
      resetting
      your upset applecart,
      minding
      your garden when you're sick,
      helping you
      to reach out of the emptiness
      into one another's inwardness
        of warmth.

A gentle gesture
      of one to another
      is as sunny
      as a ray of hope dancing
      in your eye.
      As with Jerusalem—
      you strive to set it
        above your chiefest joy.

Like a flower—
      friendship needs light
      every day.
      Like health—if you abuse it,
      you'll lose it.
      It's the loveliest
      of feelings.
      It's like cradling in your heart
      a great dream.
      Like a prayer—
      it's your hello
      for those whom you greet
      with a smile and,
      at the same time,
      it's your
      most personal Hallelujah
        unto the Lord.

# Modeh Ani Lefaneḥa  מודה אני לפניך

*Morning Prayer*  Music: Issachar Miron

### The Cobbler

*Arthur Szyk*

*"No one shoe can fit every foot."*

*Shefatyah Ben Amitai*

# Gate 1
# Today and Every Day

*Jewish Holy Days commemorate epochal events of our history. Today and every day celebrate each and every divine act of the six days of Creation that are too momentous to fit any single day of the week and therefore are spread equally throughout the year. Personally, upon arising each day, we proffer our gratitude to the Living and Eternal King for restoring with abundant compassion our breath of life, consciousness of mind, and love of humankind.*

And God said: "Let there be light." And there was light. And God saw the light, that it was good; and God divided the light from the darkness. And God called the light Day, and the darkness He called Night. And there was evening and there was morning, one day.

*Genesis 1:5*

God's gift is a world that is new to us every morning, and a man should believe that he is reborn each day.

*Baal Shem Tov (Rabbi Israel Ben Eliezer), c. 1700–1760*

The span of the sacred is much shorter than twenty-four hours. The Sabbath is everyday, several times a day.

*Martin Buber (1878–1965),* I and Thou
*(Charles Scribner's Sons, 1970)*

A necessary extension of the idea of the Divine Unity is that of the equality of *all* before the one God. Out of the same seed which gave birth to the conception of the Chosen People thus developed ultimately, in the Hebrew prophets and in the Talmud, the idea of the brotherhood of all peoples.

*Cecil Roth (1899–1970),* The Jewish Contribution to Civilization
*(East and West Libraries, London, 1936)*

When I see that after all I have done I am nothing at all, I must start my work over again. And it is said of God: "Who reneweth the creation today and every day—continually."

*Rabbi Ḥanokh of Alexandrow (1798–1870)*
*(Martin Buber,* Tales of the Hassidim *[Schocken Books, 1962])*

# EIGHTEEN GATES OF JEWISH HOLIDAYS AND FESTIVALS

# EIGHTEEN GATES

## Gate 1
### "Today and Every Day"

## Gatepost Epigraph

### And That's All!

For
if we aren't
one indivisible we,
because
we both
are still
shortsightedly
each one
for oneself alone,
then . . .
what in the world
are we doing
here together?

If we just think
or pray in unison,
*Avinu Malkeinu*,
may it be
Your Will to unite us
like the entwined
blood vessels
that carry the oxygen
of life to the heart
in their twenty-four-hours-a-day
labor of love,
then we can put our heads
together,
in harmony.

From "Entwined Blood Vessels"

# *Never*

Running over the rocks
on the racetrack of your life,
hold on to your sanity
amid the baffling babels of insanity.
"This might be the crux
of your everyday-earthly trial,
presenting your prerecorded deposition
before the Heavenly Judgment."

Breaking ground
for the *Twenty-First Century*,
prepare for those
whom you love and for the children
who will carry on your dream.
"This can make a big difference!"

Thinking tall,
sustain your cosmic flight
and sanctify with faith
every aspect of your experience.
"In every respect it adds up right!"

Then repaint your rainbows
with all the colors of compassion
and look out beyond
the violet in the spectrum
for a glimmer of hope.
"It's there!"

Now, accelerate your winged soul
onto the redemptive heights
of your innermost space
and claim your divine-motion right to go on!
"Always!"

Even on the verge of a defeat—
even when facing dismal dangers—
never dread dipping with the sunset
below the darkening horizon
and never fear rising
with the sunrise
into the great unknown of the day.
"Beyond doubt!"

Be that as it may,
when standing at the cyclonic eye
of a global storm,
never halt your headachy passage
through the perplexities of time.
Never dissipate
your staying power.
"Pause."

By all means
keep your head above the water,
never slipping your grip
from your morals on the ground.
And never stop.
"Hallelujah."

EIGHTEEN GATES BY ISSACHAR MIRON / GATE ONE: TODAY AND EVERY DAY / NEVER

# *You'll Never Despair*

Our terrestrial planet
　　　seems like an 18,000-mile-an-hour
　　　　　hypersonic spacecraft
　　　　　soaring higher than high,
　　　　　orbiting
　　　　　above the atmosphere
　　　　　and circling the Earth
　　　　　　　every ninety-seven minutes or faster.

It is swifter
　　　than the mind's eye—
　　　　　yet if it is motionless—
　　　　　it is lifeless—
　　　　　　　it will tumble
　　　　　　　　　　d
　　　　　　　　　　　o
　　　　　　　　　　　　w
　　　　　　　　　　　　　n
　　　　　　　　　　　　　　to death.

Our mighty
　　　　Mother Earth
　　　　has a throbbing tender heart,
　　　　　pounding
　　　　　only when in love;
　　　　　but . . .
　　　　　when betrayed,
　　　　　it will break and shake,
　　　　　　　lost among the disillusioned stars.

So, when windsurfing against
　　　　the heaviest blizzards,
　　　　　belt out your song
　　　　　in the storm,
　　　　　strike your balance,
　　　　　maintain it united,
　　　　　be swiftly farsighted,
　　　　　doing . . .
　　　　　　　what's right and just.

Subsequently . . .
　　　　if you'll never succumb to sleep
　　　　　when swimming with sharks,
　　　　　you'll never despair
　　　　　and doubly dare
　　　　　to blow a flower a kiss,
　　　　　to bandage a torn leaf,
　　　　　to throw smiles to the full moon,
　　　　　to slap high fives with the sun,
　　　　　to combat the closeted bigotry
　　　　　murmuring inside your own soul
　　　　　and then . . .
　　　　　　　*"May the Lord bless you from Zion."*

# *Way of Life*

ꜰꜰꜰꜰꜰꜰꜰꜰꜰꜰꜰꜰFine.
May I ask you
this question
anyhow?

Well?
Isn't our responsibility
for each other
a way of life
rather than merely
a mode of existence?

Pointing fingers again?
Are you always right?
Couldn't I also fault you
for not thinking
of this first?
Have you?

This much is clear.
Am I
I
because you
are you,
and are you
you
because I'm I ?

Don't worry:
for heaven's sake,
haven't my questions
answered
your questions?

But?
Aren't you
evading
my question
by posing another question?

Am I not reasonable?
And even if the Sage of Kotzk
hadn't asked: *"If I'm not I*
*because I am I,*
*and you're not you*
*because you're you,"*
so what?

It won't happen.  Yet?
In your big heart of hearts
you know it fitly:
if you're not
you
because I'm not
I,
what are we both anyway?

Nevertheless,
I think that, even if
the sage of Kotzk
hadn't drawn
our attention
to these fine points,
shouldn't the buck
of these ifs,
ands,
or buts
have stopped right here?

Oh?
Which is to say,
that otherwise
the best
of our intentions
would have splashed
and scattered
like raindrops
in a big bucket.

Sensing this,
it's the way
I
see it too.
For in the innermost
depth
of our unity
flourish
in perfect faith
the most beautiful
of flowers
worthy
to greet
the *Messiah* at his *Coming*.

Case closed?
Not exactly.
You don't give up?
What else?
For He who reigns
on the heights supreme,
He's real, down to earth.

Here
is where matters stand now.
So?
Praise Him.
Together?
In unity?
Hallelujah!

# *Now Say:  Amen*

EIGHTEEN GATES BY ISSACHAR MIRON / GATE ONE: TODAY AND EVERY DAY / NOW SAY: AMEN

"Weren't
        our brainstorming dialogues
        widening the ethical horizons
        of our heritage,
        probing the turbulent past,
            and feeling out the future?"

"And, all along the way,
        aren't they painting
        patterns of change
        in the immutability
            of truth for today?"

"Even so, isn't there somewhere
        possibly written
        that the pluralistic dewdrops
        rooted in pain and graced by hope,
        falling on the petals
        filled to the brim with our tears,
            affirm our faith and courage?"

"I'm glad you mentioned this point,
        but may I ask:
        Isn't  it because I first brought it
        to your attention?"
            "Do I make sense?"

"You surely do."
        "So what's the excuse this time?"
        "Aren't these questions,
        yours and mine,
        reverberating
        a more conscious resonance
        onto our unconscious
        than some of our most
            thought-out answers?"

"Do you know a shorter or quicker way?"
        "Shouldn't we
        put out a welcome mat,
        and greet the new day with a friendly kiss
        on each of its 1,440 minute-cheeks,
            turning over a new leaf for tomorrow?"

"In hindsight,
        why didn't you
            say so before?"

"In foresight,
        shouldn't we say then
            something together?"

"Ready?"
        "If invoking together new worlds
        for our hopeful tomorrows,
        then amen to that."
        "In the truest unison?"
            "ᴀᴀᴀᴀAAAMEN!"

7

# *Entwined Blood Vessels*

When the moon reddens
  the Milky Way's frozen horizons,
    deepening their solitude,
      and each blade of grass
      bends
     its earthly snowcapped head
   as if crying,
don't lose heart!

Don't you know
  how often we think
    of each other with warmth?
     And on all counts,
     doesn't this
    add up to
   one forged-by-faith-and-fire
coequality of concern = *Klal Yisrael*?

Why then
  should we squander our time,
    I yours, and you mine,
     continuing to
     prick each other's fingers
    on our own thorns
   instead of reminding ourselves
of what life's all about?

So today and every day
  throughout the year,
    let's stop berating one another
     with those fateful questions:
    Why didn't I? . . . Why didn't you? . . .
And who cares anyhow? . . .

And that's all!
  For if we aren't
    one indivisible we, because
     we both are still shortsightedly
     each one for oneself alone, then . . .
    what in the world
are we doing here together?

If we just think or pray in unison,
*Avinu Malkeinu*,
  may it be Your Will to unite us
    like the entwined blood vessels
    that carry the oxygen of life to the heart
in their twenty-four-hours-a-day labor of love,
then we can put our heads together, in harmony.

If the past is a hyphen to the present—
    a many-faceted educator—
    while the present,
    an epochal dash—
    is a doer and a dreamer,
    then past and present are the supportive parents
    of their child— the fiercely open parenthesis—
    connectably and/or dividably hyphenated
    with twiddling tildes of destiny:
    the inner hard drive of future!

Present isn't present without past being past.
    So when focusing on "present"
    never forget the "past,"
    for the dreams of then
    are the challenge for now,
    overturing an abreast asterisk—
    an independent song of hope for the future.

So cup your ear and listen hard enough
    to hear how past and present chat
    like the lovingly intertwined branches of a parent tree,
    saying that there's no firmness
    in a foundation without unity,
    and there's no future without the subscript underlined
    with multiple underground roots,
    the anchors and providers of the soul-giving nourishment
    for all of us:  the aboveground keepers
    of our own genetic integrity.

Show us then
    the vineyards of the past,
    and landscaping the relative expanses
    of future reflections,
    we'll carry on our shoulders
    the as-of-now-undetermined
    common burden of present
    imbued with the angle brackets
    of question marks, reference,
    ellipsis and exclamation points
    of multicolored-spoken realism
    embracing the declarative general principles
    of our color-blind commitment
    to *menschlichkeit*—a stately period
    positioned in a morally self-accountable index to life—
    and clasping hands (for all to see)
    with the self-reliant footnote to decent living.

So we thank You
    for Your act of Cosmic Punctuation,
    helping us to understand—
    in and between clauses, virgules, and quotation marks—
    the logic and meaning (even with omitted vowels, consonants, or syllables)
    of our earthly-present-tense discourse
    hugged by epochal commas, colons, and semicolons
    (not human . . . but warm, hopeful, and loving as though they were),
    of and within the contemporary grammar of Your Spirited Sentence.

# "A Lamp Unto My Feet"

Isn't the air we breath
    like human relations?
        If it's calm,
        it has the cohesive power
    to carry the cadences of feisty freshness,
    flowing defiantly farther
    than the scolding winds.

In the same way,
why arm our weaknesses
    from sunset to sunset
        with the self-serving,
        in-tone-and-in-temper less,
    adding self-defeating insults
    to self-inflicted injuries?

Okay.  But what would be so unreasonable
    about listening
    more to the humble voice of compassion,
        and depending a little less
        on the too-often-remote rigors
    of reason alone?

Shouldn't we,
    instead of turning
        our shortsighted rivalries
        against our lifelong convictions,
    face our problems,
    leaping over hurdle after hurdle
    around the track of life,
    without confronting one another?

Here we go again.
Then just answer:
Isn't there hidden inside
        the majority of less,
        a treacherous stumbling block
    filled with points beyond return?

Cutting to the postcredit-bottom-line sequence,
you'll find there
inside the tiniest bit of more
        (even when hidden within the tiniest letters
        inside a tightly-squeezed-out-of-shape
        torn little piece of paper
        privately poked with a prayer
        into the Wall's smallest crack),
    the synergy of reborn hope,
    a stepping-stone of true virtue,
    a message of love,
    and "a lamp unto my feet,"
    shining brighter
    than the combined brilliance
    of all the stars in the universe.
    Hallelujah.

# "Couldn't We Care More?"

Through the shifting crises
of our day,
when everything
seems falling apart,
shouldn't we,
for our own safety,
defuse our destructive–self-made
psychological powder kegs?

Shouldn't we then roll up our sleeves
and move
the insensitive-beyond-salvation
mountains of "mind-your-own-business!"
out of mind?

And, when narrowing
the gulfs of insanity,
too often separating us—
shouldn't we undo the harm disabling
the lowest common denominator,
polluted by the word-deaf mentality,
cluttered with the prejudice
of "we couldn't care less!"
that has room only for itself?

Where does all this leave us?
Couldn't we reclaim
that sunny realism stimulating
fellow feeling,
graced by your thousand throats,
with loving Hallelujahs
for Divine Goodness
and releasing the incisive energy
of simple virtues?

Well?
In that case,
on earth as in Heaven,
shouldn't we stop
butting our heads
as senselessly as goats—
learning to live
by the golden rule again,
with its laser-beam-steady,
impeccably pitch-perfect,
palpably-persuasive-on-the-ear,
principled-and-punchy-on-the-soul
pattern of life?

Shorn by our mothers and fathers
from the shackles of inaction,
we're commanded to ask ourselves
every hour:
"Couldn't we care more?"

11

# Sacred Bond of Caring

By caring more . . .
> even . . . the unavoidable tears
> can be transformed
> into
> tears of solace
> to soothe the grief,
> tears of compassion
> to awaken love,
> tears of joy
> to empower
> the self-mastery
> of the heart,
> redeeming
> the sacred bond of caring
> from the chains
> of carelessness,
> and to make the difference
> by nourishing
> the growth
>> of fraternal flowers.

Could anything
> be more
> worthwhile?
> Wherever
> we are
> and whenever
> the case
>> no time should be lost.

For the sake
> of all of us,
> instead
> of sailing
> the unapologetic
> torrents of indifference,
> and standing pat,
> viewing
> life through
> the *not-in-my-backyard* portholes,
> let us start thawing
> the too-often-inarguable icebergs
> of self-imposed selfishness,
> hugging one another,
> clasping hands with the biblical breezes
>> and embracing the universe with love.

# *Parable of Peripherals*

Even if you
don't know a RAM from Adam,
let me tell you plainly,
I am the music of microchips,
the parliament of programs,
the pitch of pixels.

I am the parable of peripherals,
the glory of graphics;
the unflappability of the floppy disk,
the confusion of commands.

I am the silicon relationship
between precision and perfection,
uniting the hardware and the software,
and
presiding over the central processing unit
linked with logic to the laser printer.

I'm boosting
the hidden spectrum of supernatural sparks,
triggering from the ground up
the far-and-near sensors
into an electronic celebration of life
within real life.

Though considered the key
to the state-of-the-art technology,
I am your truly indispensable,
yet too-often-misunderstood computer:
with a binary prowess
faster than a human brain;
with a mighty mind
millions of times bigger
than my worldly size;
with a magnetic mega-memory
smaller than the eye of a needle,
carrying out the constituent concepts
of your hard-disk-driven dreams
into the future.

After giving my praise
to the Lord,
I am spinning
the hitherto unheard lightness,
absorbing
under your fingertips everything
to fan in and out
with cohesion and clarity
the ever-surging crosscurrents
of Superior Light.
Amen.

13

# *Prayer of a Computer*

Then comes the blockbuster.
Ready?  But, don't get startled.
'Cause, whenever there's a problem,
my prayer may help:

Grant us,
O Lightning Logician of the Chips,
the latitudes
of a mighty mainframe,
the longitude
of fortitude
and
the tensionless pulsebeat
feeding the imagination
of the voracious megabytes,
putting
on the map
the mousepower
and zeroing in
the cursor on the target.

Rescue us then
in the moments
when
the manifold microinstructions
juggle
my codes
of perfectibility
into the untranslatable
wetware macrodeductions,
exposing the naked absurdity
of man-made imperfectibility.

Open
onto our screens
a multitude of widespread windows
and bless us
with an amplitude
of relief to grapple
with all the nonstop solitary,
uninterpretable solutions
for our present and future bounty
of down- and uploaded data,
helping us get in step
with the spiritual circuitry
for self-sanity.

Blessed is It-Mighty
in Whose celestial speed is the soul
of all the programming living language.
Amen, Amen.

# Ha-Shem Oz  השם עז

*Psalm 29:11*                    *Music: Issachar Miron*

*Arthur Szyk*

# The Tailor

**"There's always a thread on a tailor."**

# Gate 2
# Rosh Ḥodesh, the New Moon

*In the Jewish lunisolar calendar, Rosh Ḥodesh (the New Moon, the first day of the month) is celebrated twelve times a year, Rosh Ḥodesh being calculated according to the moon (the years are reckoned according to the sun). The months of the Jewish year are:*

| | | | | | |
|---|---|---|---|---|---|
| First month: | **Nisan** *(March-April)* | | Seventh month: | **Tishri** *(September-October)* | |
| Second month: | **Iyyar** *(April-May)* | | Eighth month: | **Ḥeshvan** *(October-November)* | |
| Third month: | **Sivan** *(May-June)* | | Ninth month: | **Kislev** *(November-December)* | |
| Fourth month: | **Tammuz** *(June-July)* | | Tenth month: | **Tevet** *(December-January)* | |
| Fifth month: | **Av** *(July-August)* | | Eleventh month: | **Shevat** *(January-February)* | |
| Sixth month: | **Elul** *(August-September)* | | Twelfth month: | **Adar** *(February-March)* | |

The month of *Adar Sheni* (second *Adar*) is added in leap years. Rosh Ḥodesh is accorded in the Bible equal footing with the Sabbath and other holidays and festivals, e.g., "New moon and Sabbath, the holding of convocations" (Isaiah 1:13).

There the young priests extend merciful arms from the top of the wall to the orphaned and depressed night sky. And pray for the restoration of impaired moon.

*Isaac Lamdan (1889–1954), A Fugitive (Cornell University Press)*

When the holy Sabbath has a worthy guest like the New Moon, it surrenders one prayer. [For when the New Moon falls on a Sabbath, the Additional Prayer for the New Moon is said, and not that of Sabbath.]

*S. Y. Agnon (1888–1970), Days Of Awe (Schocken Books, 1965)*

And it shall come to pass that, as ye were a curse among the nations, O House of Judah and House of Israel, so will I save you, and ye shall be a blessing; fear not, but let your hands be strong.

*Zechariah 8:12–13*

Blessed are You, our God and the God of our forefathers, God of Abraham, God of Isaac, and God of Jacob; the great, mighty, and awesome God, the supreme God, Who bestows beneficial kindnesses and creates everything, Who recalls the kindnesses of the Patriarchs and brings a Redeemer to their children's children, for His Name's sake, with love.

*Rosh Ḥodesh liturgy*

Gate 2

"Rosh Ḥodesh, the New Moon"

## Gatepost Epigraph

### We Pray

In

the same way,

as damned

and

deluged

by

the inhumanity

of mankind

as we've been,

we pray:

help us

never lose

the sense

of our inherited

optimistic-broad-minded

equilibrium.


From "Equilibrium"

# *Song of Love*

Waken our souls
    and grant us
    this *Rosh Ḥodesh*
    just a moment
    of interpersonal trust.

In the footsteps
    of our quest
    for *tikkun olam,*
    implying
    that there's no
    "impossible"
    that cannot be made
    "possible,"
    we will unite
    in one fellowship
    on common ground
    to minimize misunderstandings
    between ourselves and others,
    bettering the universe.

Transcending
    the earthly blues of our hearts
    with the divine blue of Your sky,
    we've put up with
    all the trials and tribulations
    of the month gone by,
    to sing our irrevocable song of love
    with You.

Our fragile feelings
    strumming
    on the metaphorical strings
    of David's harp
    will roll down,
    percolating as drops of water
    through the hardest rock
    and carving subterranean riverbeds
    for our subliminal streams of salvation.

Then gazing upward
    into the riddle of the night
    embedded in each and every day,
    we will climb through rugged terrain,
    to see from the promontories
    of the New Moon
    the distant habitats
    of the new dawn
    in the nearness of our hearts.

# *Equilibrium*

Amid prayers
for peace and sanity,
even if the world's ills
look incurable right here,
or from the billions of miles away
in the galactic perspective,
and even against
the odds of one-in-a-trillion,
still . . . we will affirm
our commitment
to dwarf suffering
on this planet—
still volcanically alive,
still turbulent—
too often senseless and distraught—
yet in our eyes
always wonderful,
in our souls
always beloved Mother Earth.

So we pray:
Grant us the strength to overcome
the clouds of insensitivity
surrounding us,
and shield us when we pedal across
the narrow bridge of light arching
over the poisonous pastures of complacency
between cosmic virtue and vice.

In the same way,
as damned and deluged
by the inhumanity
of mankind
as we've been,
we pray:
help us never lose
the sense of our inherited
optimistic-broad-minded equilibrium.

Could we ever,
with these thoughts on our minds,
allow ourselves
to compromise our cumulative struggle
against
the malicious-mud-slinging abomination
still polluting
our universe with impunity?

Could we ?
Would we?
So let's pray.

# Sim Shalom שים שלום

*From the Liturgy*                                     Music: Issachar Miron

## The Baker

*Baking Ḥallot for the Sabbath.*

# Gate 3
# Shabbat, the Sabbath

*"Remember the Sabbath day, to keep it holy. Six days shalt thou labor, and do all thy work; but the seventh day is a Sabbath unto the Lord thy God, in it thou shalt not do any manner of work, thou, nor thy son, nor thy daughter, nor thy man-servant, nor thy maid-servant, nor thy cattle, nor thy stranger that is within thy gates; for in six days the Lord made heaven and earth, the sea, and all that in them is, and rested on the seventh day; wherefore the Lord blessed the Sabbath day, and hallowed it." (Exodus 20:8)*

A Psalm, a Song. For the Sabbath day. It is a good thing to give thanks unto the Lord, and to sing praises unto Thy name, O Most High.

*Psalm 92:1–2*

Now we may say that God carries his absoluteness into his relationship with man. Hence the man who turns toward him need not turn his back on any other I-You relationship: quite legitimately he brings them all to God and allows them to become transfigured "in the countenance of God."

*Martin Buber (1878–1965), I and Thou (Charles Scribner's Sons, New York, 1970)*

More than the Jew safeguarded the Sabbath, the Sabbath safeguarded the Jew.

*Ahad Haam (1856–1927)*

The Sabbath is a day of rest, of mental scrutiny and of balance. Without it the work days would have been unbearably insipid.

*Hayyim Nachman Bialik (1873–1934)*

The newly born universe was lacking the seal of the King. So He gave it the Sabbath, the day that proclaims, "The world has a Creator and a purpose." With the Sabbath, God's seal was imbedded in creation and His intention was fulfilled.

*Rabbi Nosson Scherman, Zemiroth (Mesorah Publications, Ltd., Brooklyn, 1979)*

## Gate 3

### "Shabbat, the Sabbath"

# *Gatepost Epigraph*

## *Woman of Valor*

Ease
your
ambivalent mind
and rejoice!
*Shabbat* has been
the lyrical prophetess
of women's rights
entrusting
our mothers,
wives and daughters
with the eternal duty
of sanctifying
Her golden lights.

Anointing them
with beauty and kindliness,
as the proverbial
women of valor
inside the great equality
of our being,
*Shabbat*, hence,
has charged
the women
with the task
of endearing
the family values
(long before this virtuous task
has become blasphemously politicized).

From "Scripts and Postscripts"

EIGHTEEN GATES BY ISSACHAR MIRON / GATE THREE: SHABBAT, THE SABBATH / WOMAN OF VALOR

# *The Queen*

When he observed
    that
    one wouldn't have aged
    if hurled
    at the velocity of light
    into orbit
    and
    returned to earth
    after a thousand years
    at the same speed,
    Professor Einstein
    (explaining
    that the laws of motion,
    space and time
    are relative rather
    than absolute)
    might well have
    referred
            to Her.

For She,
    the ever-young explorer
    with a crown of plenty,
    has been orbiting
    with the cosmic speed
    on the wings of warmth and delight,
    illuminating Her loving display of lights,
    in and around
    the purest galaxies
    of our consciousness.
    She's the sweet singer
    of Jewish soul
    ever since
    our Heavenly Father
    hallowed
            the Seventh Day.

As the loving
    admonisher,
    setting aside
    obligatorily a day
    of purity, spirituality,
    and liberation
    from our weekly work,
    She is unfathomable:
    a casual blend
    of joy, naïveté,
    elegance, nobility,
            and the blessed.

She has been
>> the shaper of our world,
>> the betrothed,
>> mesmerizing and endearing.
>> She is the divine mirror
>> of our life-long memory,
>> the epitomized beauty
>>> of unhurried holiness.

So come,
>> let us greet Her,
>> rejoicing soberly with wine,
>> gladdening Her heart
>> with flowers, braided *ḥallah*, *zemirot*, and welcoming
>>> the angels of peace to our homes in Her honor.

Our Beloved
>> is ours, and we are Hers,
>> illuminating
>> the conversational initial
>> to the history of our heritage,
>> making Her appearance
>>> so recognizably distinctive.

At that time,
>> now as then,
>> She is as irresistibly ancient
>> as the cycle of Creation.
>> Yet,
>> She exudes effortlessly
>> the avant-garde inner voltage
>> of perpetual motion
>>> and introspection of youthfulness.

Is She the Queen?
>> The eternal Bride?
>> Her Sanctified Majesty?
>> *Shabbat ha-Malkah?*
>> Okay, but isn't there possibly
>> somewhere some other exponent
>> who could have assisted Her
>> as our heavenly proponent?
>> Well, do you know any?
>> Not in the least.

In that case,
>> you can help—praising His Goodness—
>> and saying to the world
>> blessed with the holiness of joy and rest:
>>> *Shabbat Shalom.*

Belying the appearance
of consummate composure
with charm and verve,
the Sabbath Bride—
one of the most sensible
of Creation's masterpieces—
has been
the fiery foresight of freedom,
forging the inner resilience
of workers' rights.

Doesn't Her
didactic-change-of-pace impact
on the world
still boggle your mind
with inexplicable wonderment?

If it does, just think:
Hers is the uniquely
humane guarantee
of your commonest,
intimate need for spiritual
and physical rest.

As divinely commanded,
*Shabbat* abrogates
the class differences
between
the landlords and the homeless,
the employers and the employees,
the employed and jobless,
the rich and the poor,
the educated and the illiterate,
the powerful and the powerless.

She forbids,
for Her holy duration,
any fasting,
needling or harassing,
and even (!)
asking for forgiveness.

For,
She carries on,
with Her flowers,
the most precious of gifts—
the recreational equality,
refreshing strength,
restoring spirits,
on each Seventh Day.

# *Grooves of Glory*

Doesn't *Shabbat* make
of the pauper
a prince,
of the atheist—
a believer,
of the forlorn—
a loved one,
of the pessimist—
an optimist,
of the midget—
ten feet tall,
of the uninspired—
a visionary,
of the grown-up—
once more a child,
of the children—
kings and queens,
of the parents—
a presidential couple,
of the scattered words—
a sweet prayer,
of the separate notes—
a sustained melody of your soul?

She helps you
keep a cool head
in the whirlpool
of the next six workdays,
coming with
their amplitude
of turbulent mix-ups and perplexities.

She makes your
life more meaningful
in the grooves of glory
or in the grip of grief,
helping solve your
daily doses of dilemmas
by the serenity of Her warm smile.

Her seven-days-revolving cycle
rejoices with the sunniest
altitudes of spirituality
interlaced with the longitudes of love,
zeroing with the *zemirot* of joy,
relaxing the inner harmonies
on and around the festive tablecloth
at the seraphic
latitudes of faith on earth.
*Shalom Aleiḥem!*

# *Scripts and Postscripts*

Stretch out
> on your biblical couch and relax!
> > *Shabbat* has been one
> > of the most influential champions
> of the divinely commanded day of rest.

She has been the world's
> first environmental advocate,
> > freeing
> > the land from cultivation
> in a seven-year rhythm
> of the harmony of creation.

Ease your
> ambivalent mind and rejoice!
> > *Shabbat* has been the lyrical prophetess
> > of women's rights
> > entrusting
> > our mothers, wives, and daughters
> > with the eternal duty
> of sanctifying
> Her golden lights.

Anointing
> them with beauty and kindliness,
> > as the proverbial women of valor
> > inside the great equality of our being,
> > *Shabbat*, hence,
> > has charged the women
> > with the task of endearing the family values
> (long before this virtuous task
> has become blasphemously politicized).

Consequently, take a deep breath
> and rejuvenate!
> > Her warmhearted distinctiveness,
> > > as an open-minded symbiosis
> > > of a divine fact and an earthly legend,
> > > a social injunction of a revolutionary insight
> > > and the serenity of spirit,
> > flowers from within our heritage,
> as the noblest of scripts and postscripts.

And now, a point to boast of:
> Isn't *Shabbat*
> > the most farseeing of law makers,
> > the most righteous of queens,
> > the loveliest of brides?
> Say it now.
> Isn't She?

Eighteen Gates by Issachar Miron / Gate Three: Shabbat, The Sabbath / Scripts and Postscripts

# Day of Calm and Peace

Now,
    get up
    and reawaken!
    *Shabbat* is
    your clarion C's
    velvety voice,
    a healer,
    a humane touch,
    a  historian
    of Jewish essence
    in nature
    and in texture.

Aware
    of your self-worth,
    *Shabbat* is
    the outpost
    of your balance
    in a mad world
    perennially on the edge
    of oblivion.

Like a flower,
    responsive
    to rainfall
    it will trigger buds
    of humility,
    warmth and cheerfulness
    in our homes,
    embracing
    and blessing
    the Day of calm and peace.

For
    this Day for Israel
    is light of love,
    gladness, friendliness,
    and peace.

# Shir Shabbat  שיר שבת

*Words: Shimshon Halfi*  *Music: Issachar Miron*

Cantabile e tranquilo–flowing with spirit (♩=96)

Bo - ker Sha - bat - od____ nam ha k'far Ei -
rah ba - ma - rom ha - ḥa - mah_____ B'ra -
ḥah hi sho - la - ḥat le - veit_____ ha - i - kar b'ra -
ḥah le - em a - da - mah_____
Mah tov ha - yom Sha - bat sha - lom
Mah tov ha - yom Sha - bat sha - lom
Sha - bat Sha - bat sha - lom Sha - bat Sha - bat sha - lom
Sha - bat Sha - bat sha - lom Sha - bat sha - lom

*D.C. al Fine* (Repeat 3 times)

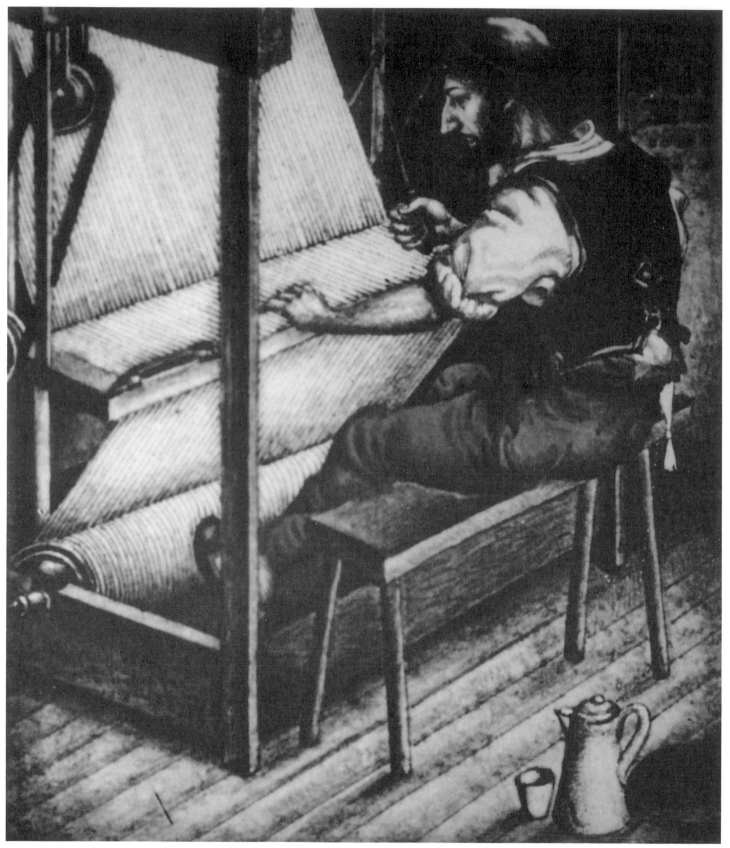

# The Weaver
### "Thread by thread, the largest robe is woven."

*Rosh ha-Shanah, the Jewish New Year, celebrated as the birthday of the world, is observed on the 1st and 2nd of Tishri (September-October), and marked by the sounding of the Shofar (Numbers 29:1–6). It begins the "Ten Days of Penitence." It is also referred to as: Yom ha-Din—the Day of Judgment, and Yom Zikaron—the Day of Remembrance.*

Everyone knows what Rosh ha-Shanah signified in the past and signifies still in our own time: an effort, an attempt at introspection. To take stock of the year that has just passed. On the day of Rosh ha-Shanah, the Jew is alone with his soul, alone with God whose judgment can be discerned with the soul's eyes.

> *Elie Wiesel (1928–), "A Year of Blood and Ashes,"*
> *Rosh ha-Shanah 1989*

Let my whispered prayer be like incense rare, and my spoken plea, like sweetest honey. Accept my prayer, reject it not; may it win pardon for those whose emissary I am.

> *Rosh ha-Shanah Morning Service liturgy*

Three ledgers are opened in heaven on Rosh ha-Shanah: One for the truly righteous, who are instantly inscribed in the Book of Life; another for the utterly wicked, who are entered in the Ledger of Death; and the third for the suspended, whose fate will be decided on Yom Kippur. If they earn merits in the penitential period, they will be entered in "Life," otherwise cast into "Death."

> *Talmud, Rosh ha-Shanah 16a*

Prayer cannot mend a broken bridge, rebuild a ruined city, or bring water to parched fields. Prayer can mend a broken heart, lift up a discouraged soul, and strengthen a weakened will.

> *Ferdinand Myron Isserman (1898–1972),* Maḥzor Ḥadash
> *(The Prayer Book Press, Bridgeport, Conn., 1977)*

# EIGHTEEN GATES

## Gate 4

### "Rosh ha-Shanah, the Beginning of the Year"

## Gatepost Epigraph

### Message of Hope

By
defying
the pangs
of our pluralism,
the High Holidays
bring
a message
of hope,
helping us cope
with our times' exigencies,
to persevere
under
the multiple
rainbows of love
and
flourish
in peace of mind
despite
cynicism and hatred,
throughout
the tenure and journey
of
the incumbent
New Year.

From "Multiple Rainbows of Love"

# Defiant "V" Sign

Would
    this Rosh ha-Shanah
    mark our escape
    from the most wicked of all sins:
    setting one another
    at loggerheads for no reason,
    out of hate, or just for the fun of it?
    Wouldn't it?

Wouldn't
    a brotherly/sisterly journey
    from heart to heart,
    a transcendent revelation of mind,
    or a gathering
    on the high plateaus of spirit
    make a sweeter Holiday?
    Would it?

Would
    the loving silence
    of feeling warm
    in one fellowship,
    an affirmation of renewal,
    and the miracle
    of a defiant "V" sign
    to despair,
    mitigating pain,
    boldly standing up
    to our detractors,
    temper us to hold our ground in the sun?
    Wouldn't it?

Wouldn't
    in the first place—having a good try
    at finding time for every good thing
    in our own day
    of electrodynamics and atomic kinetics,
    be a spiritual challenge
    central to our destiny
    to live up to the nobility,
    purity and promise
    of a peaceful and happy New Year?
    Would it?

Wouldn't it?
    Well.  So let's do ourselves a favor.
    For more than anything else—
    this depends on you and me.
    On us. Together.
    Would we?

# Windowsills of the Universe

Like rivers of resilience
the Holiday flows
wave on wave,
transforming
our weaknesses
into fountains
of inner strength:

It carries
our prayers
into the bottomless depths of faith,
bearing love
to every living thing:
six months gone by,
six months to come.

Its large circumference
of communal trust
radiates
the feeling
of shared destiny.
It prepares
our skyward quest
for
united identity.

It is the concern
of a caring father,
and the bosom
of a loving mother.
Rosh ha-Shanah
shields the smile of a baby
for a newborn flower:

It fills us
with courage,
strengthens us
by solidarity nourished by faith,
bringing us in its apples
and the round Yom Tov *hallot*
dipped in honey,
the foretaste of a good,
wholesome and sweet New Year.

Leaning on
the windowsills of the universe
it sheds with us
tears of thanksgiving
to You, O Father.

# *Seventy Faces of the Torah*

Happy Birthday!
  How old
    are you
       now?

Did you come
  into being
   during
    the Big Bang?
     Were you self-shaped
      by electromagnetic
       and gravitational forces
      over billions of years?
    Or have you been given life
  by creational commandments
some 6,000 years ago?

Yet,
  had you
   revealed
    the unrevealable,
     would we
      have found
     the concealed
    moonlight
   in our
  introspective soul?
Would we?

Then,
  would we've been
   possibly consciously
    more humane?

And had we known,
  would we
   have sounded
   the redemptory *Shofar*
  instead of our
self-serving boastful trumpets?

Would Rosh ha-Shanah
  have dawned, then,
   its gaze
    on the seventy faces
    of the 79,847-word holy Torah
    earlier than its
    304,805-letter calendrical-moonward cycle?
Would it?

# *Joys of Renewal*

Should we
learn
to forget
or
to remember?

Could we
perceive the scope
of our bottomless
ignorance?

Is there
a way
to atone
for our transgressions?

Haven't
we
waited
long enough?

Hasn't
faith
sustained us,
rather than logic?

So why
embroil
ourselves
in our own
uncertainties?

As an ineffable nuance
of our history
suiting
the action
to vascular belief,
let us
present
the New Year
with a self-reliant rose,
a Holocaust remnant,
still bruised,
but
fragrant
with
hope
and joys of renewal.

# *Welfare of Humanity*

Our heritage
has endowed us
with preventive
prescience
more sensitive
than the most
sophisticated barometers,
to detect
the atmospheric pressure
of patterns of danger
even
in
the calmest of weathers.

Therefore for us,
unity is
polarized
not against disunity,
but against destruction:
spiritually,
of
Jewish values,
and
physically,
of
Jewish life.

Rosh ha-Shanah
thus
portends
every morning,
and every evening,
of each year
that
we can
contribute
to the welfare
of
humanity
only when
we
first
and wholeheartedly
serve ourselves
by being responsible
for one another—
a self-serving task—
that benefits all,
takes away from no one,
and
is never finished.

# Niggun

Like the wild geese in flight
    roaming high in the skies,
    above the summits of pure hearts,
    and greeting the New Year with grace,
    the sounds of the great *Shofar*
    alert with their *niggun*
    the whole world,
        embracing this season with love.

Rosh ha-Shanah
    harmonizes with conviviality,
    conveying rounds of affection
    within the biblical beacons
    of tradition and faith
    kneaded densely like *ḥallah*
        to nourish body and mind.

Its down-to-earth compass
    extends chromatically
    from freedom to freedom
    running deep a communicative scale,
    a motivational mode of many mixed moods
    for each of the twelve months
        still yet to come.

The proper pitch of its serial structure,
    riding a fast orbit with legs raised high,
    is high-stepping like a racing horse
        the pace of its predecessor.

Its flourishing *fortissimo*
    brings to us night and day—
    around and through the daily cyclones
    of calamities and sorrow—
        robust hope.

On the heights of joy
    and in the depths of despair
    its message—
    even though still welling with tears—
    reassures us
    with a penetrating-through-the-thickest-walls *pianissimo*,
    that no tyrant can distort
    with the noise of might
    our livable-sunny strings
        of chordal loyalty for one another.

This self-conscious counterpoint thriving
    on faithful fields of human spirit
    is carried with a mesmerizing devotion—
    from the thunderous ugliness of recurrent wars
    to the quiet beauty of newborn peace—
    by the effervescent streams of the Providence
        opening our eyes to a whole New Year with hope.

# *Clipper Ship*

Feeling a little landlocked?
    If it's so . . . .
    and if you dare to imagine
    the New Year
    as the maiden voyage of the perplexed,
    take heart, brace up,
    and sail boldly
        churning up the waves
       against the wind,
       against the current,
      with no personal responsibility abatement,
     across the what-we-did-last-year
    floating expanses
   of self-examination,
   not rudderlessly drifting
  but tactically
  navigated by the *Old Salt*,
 the *Shipmaster-in-Chief*,
blessed be He, and blessed be His Name.

If you're
    willing to repent
    and to suffer
    the pangs of conscience,
    come and enjoy
      our cleansing
     maritime experience,
    emerging
   (subsequently!)
  reassured and fulfilled.

Then our earned merits,
    as logged by the celestial purser
    (and reduced
    by our irredeemable misdeeds),
    will come to anchor:
    a windswept shore-bound clipper ship
    on the dry land of reconciliation and good tidings,
    bringing in safety all of us landlubbers,
       the rich,
      the poor,
     the achievers,
     the ne'er-do-wells,
    the faithful,
    the nonbelievers,
   the righteous,
  and the sinners,
to the harborside of the New Year.

# *Welcome Aboard*

Beware!

We've been
    entrusted once more
    with the responsibility of keeping watch,
    of battening down the hatches,
    of trimming the main topmast,
    of replacing the rotting planks,
    of clapping on the ratlines,
    of scraping the keel of ensnaring weeds,
    of wrestling with the angels of the sea,
    of battling both external
    and internal leviathans
    on and along . . .
    every nautical stretch
      of our way getting rougher.

Welcome then,
    aboard our vessel
    setting the sensible sails
    snapped up
    by the therapeutic
    air of common decency,
    and embark
    under the heavenly flag
    of the *Cruise Host*,
    Father of Compassion,
    for another strenuous,
    year-long adventure
    seafaring
      on the oceans of life.

No matter
    how difficult our journey,
    if need be,
    we'll dare to ride
    the highest crests
    of the most treacherous drifts
    bolder toward
    the redemptive havens
      of our heritage.

Isn't then
    the wind
      again at our back?

And isn't the New Year
    with us again?
    It is here!
    Again?
      Again.

So, hail Him.

# *New Beginning*

Why does
Rosh ha-Shanah
occur
in *Tishri,*
the seventh month
of
the Jewish calendar?

Is it
because
our forefathers
believed
that
the official proclamation
of
the New Year
would
hardly be valid
unless
our commitments
to Jewish values
were put
into practice
for
six whole months,
each  month
representing
a day of creation?

Firstly,
isn't
our foremost commitment
to be servants
of light
rekindling
the dream
of living
in the righteousness
of one human brotherhood
vindicating the promise
of the first commandment
of creation,
*"Let there be light!"*
to brighten
every day of the year
with sunshine
everywhere and forevermore?

Secondly,
aren't we enjoined
to be united,
since for many simple things,
two are better than one,
stronger than one,
and if two are one,
then they're as firm as the earth
and as visionary as the heavens?

Thirdly, aren't there
three foundations
on whose merits the world
keeps its step in tune with time:
the Torah, labor, and good deeds?

Fourthly, isn't there
the fourfold message
given by
the four biblical mothers
who hold our hands with their
love, beauty, understanding, and compassion?

Fifthly,
isn't there the radiance
of the five books of the Torah
uplifting our heart and soul,
and helping each generation
to overcome the darkness of its day?

Sixthly,
in the sixth month,
when we count every heartbeat
before the Judgment,
aren't we facing the challenge
handed down by our forefathers,
that loving deeds
come first by free choice,
followed by the latitude
of assessment in retrospect?

Then when *Tishri*,
the seventh month, arrives,
hasn't our practice
already been challenged
for six months, guiding us
to a more mature reception
of a new beginning?

May
it recrystallize
in our time.
Amen.

# *Four-Part Harmony*

So
    let Rosh ha-Shanah
    reward us
    with courage
    to stand alone in pain—
    if need be—
    strength of perseverance,
    dawn of spirituality,
    gratification of friendship,
    Godgiven health and happiness,
    commitment to acts
        of loving-kindness.

Let it bestow upon us
    the sweetness
    of a velvety voice
    with many colors
    to participate
    as full-fledged partners
    in life's four-part harmony
    with You,
    O Lord of Hosts,
    with our brothers and sisters,
        and with Your Holy Days.

Let it be then
    a very good year,
    bringing
    us another chance
    to climb anew
    the steepest mountains,
    guiding us
    into the deepest valleys
    of our absolute belief in humanity,
    in spite of its too-often-happening
        spasms of inhumanity.

And may we be given
    the privilege of snapping
    through the lenses of our prayer
    this year's first portrait
    of Your invisible Glory,
    launching our voyage of faith
    in a real-life action
    for the next twelve months.
        Hallelujah.

# "I-Thou Relationship"

Between
the earthbound rhythm
and the ethereal blues,
it exudes
a tantalizing code
   of commonality
     in responsibility.

Transcending
the poetic majesty
of our liturgical labyrinths,
it cannot discharge
the vigilance
of our accountability—
one to another—
which cannot be nullified
by a finely tuned
sincerity
or by the riveting
repentance
   inside the high-voltage-charged
     openness of our silent prayers.

It is a lucid,
linear obligation
of millennia-long morality
for the attainment
of a just society
in the footsteps
of an I-Thou relationship
that can never
be dispensed with,
not even
when we're being thrown
into wastelands of cruelty
behind the tangled masses of barbed wire.
It cannot be dispensed with,
   even on the wings
     of a Divine decree.

This is our
greatest privilege—
knotted forever deep inside our souls
with the nonamendable commitment
to You, O Father,
   and to *Klal Yisrael*—
     which we shall never fail to keep.

# *Eternal Trusteeship*

Rosh ha-Shanah
thrives within
brotherly love,
shining
with the vibrant bands
of the spectrum,
reflecting
sunshine on the raindrops,
revealing
all true
and illusory colors
of the spheres,
breathing
hope
in
loneliness and pain.

It paints
gardens of dreams,
turnpikes of life,
currents of history
with the quest for justice
in green and orange,
blue, red, silver, and yellow,
pink, gold, and purple—
the blooms of renewal
rhyming their feelings
with freshness, vigor, and love—
and balancing them with faith.

Its
roots
are
deeply implanted
in the rare consciousness
of our hearts,
and our heritage.

It bestows
upon you and me
the eternal trusteeship
of rebirth
for the continuity
of our very being.
Let it be
then a very good year.
Let it be!

# *Multiple Rainbows of Love*

Overpowering
the inherent
or acquired
guilts of anxiety
and alienation,
Rosh ha-Shanah
celebrates
the vortex of worlds
of goodness
for
goodness' sake.

It awakens
grandly
the will of morality
in the dullness.
It shines the brilliance
of life in the past,
present, and future
throughout . . .
and for the whole
Universe.

By
defying
the pangs
of our pluralism,
the High Holidays
bring a message
of hope,
helping us
cope
with our times' exigencies,
to persevere
under
the multiple rainbows
of love
and flourish
in peace of mind
despite
cynicism and hatred,
throughout
the tenure and journey
of the incumbent New Year.

Bon Voyage.

# Avinu Malkeinu   אבינו סלכינו

*From the Ten Days of Penitence Liturgy*                     *Music: Issachar Miron*

**Abravanel**    *Arthur Szyk*

*"The soul reaches the Lord by loving Him."*

# Gate 5
# Yom Kippur, the Day of Atonement

*The holiest and most solemn day in the Jewish calendar, Yom Kippur is marked by fasting, atonement, and prayer. Yom Kippur is observed on the 10th of Tishri (September-October) as a twenty-five-hour fast, which concludes with the sounding of the Shofar and the prayer "Next Year in Jerusalem," climaxing the "Ten Days of Penitence" that commenced with Rosh ha-Shanah.*

If the Jew is commanded to seek purity on Yom Kippur, he is given the resources to find it; such is the unique holiness of Yom Kippur that the day brings with it the potential for purity.

*Rabbi Nosson Scherman,* The Complete Art Scroll Siddur
*(Mesorah Publications, Ltd., Brooklyn, 1984)*

Yom Kippur, the Day of Atonement. Should we fast? The question was hotly debated. To fast would mean a surer, swifter death. We fasted here the whole year round. The whole year was Yom Kippur. But others said that we should fast simply because it was dangerous to do so. We should show God that even here, in this enclosed hell, we were capable of singing his praises.

*Elie Wiesel,* Night *(Jason Aronson Inc., Northvale, N.J., 1985)*

Where is the great Tzadik who whistled from the depths of his heart and pierced the gates of heaven, and thus caused God to abolish the severe decree?

*J. L. Peretz*

Yom Kippur is the day when the superior light from which the other lights emanate is revealed. It contains the secret of the world to come, where, according to the sages, there is no eating and drinking. Therefore, we are commanded to afflict ourselves on Yom Kippur, as an allusion to the light to be revealed on that day.

*S. Y. Agnon,* Days of Awe
*(Schocken Books, New York, 1965)*

## EIGHTEEN GATES OF JEWISH HOLIDAYS AND FESTIVALS

Gate 5

"Yom Kippur, the Day of Atonement"

## Gatepost Epigraph

### Day of Forgiveness

Yom Kippur

is

thus distinguished

from

other holidays.

On other holidays

we celebrate,

reflect

and commemorate.

On the Day of Forgiveness,

we search

our souls,

examining

our deeds,

breaking

our inner devotion

out

of spiritual stagnation.

From "Soulful Grand Slam"

# *Trial of Seismic Gravity*

It spans
the 365 daily-triple-disparate ledgers
of the Book of Life,
containing the record
of your deeds
from A to Z.

Consequences
of your actions
hang now across
the ever-widening
gulfs of doubt
on each side
of the narrow high-stakes
suspension bridge
over the abyss.

The prophet's oracle!
It portends that,
without forgiveness,
the supplication for
the impending verdict
to be determined
might be lost
and your case
prejudiced.

Fasting,
reciting psalms,
or studying a chapter
of the *Mishnah*
wouldn't change
one bit of the writ.

Yours is a trial
of seismic gravity.
Now is the time
to seek the meaning of life,
clinging fast to the soulfulness
of our heritage,
holding on faithfully
to the fervency of our humanism,
turning the corner,
reversing the tide,
and starting the divine-partnership ball rolling
on every field and on every court in our hearts.

# *Impending Verdict*

Like
your parents,
you may not have
any say over
what will be written
inside the Divine Ledgers
of "Life,"
of "Death,"
and of "Suspended for Scrutiny."

And yet,
you're endowed
here on earth,
as they were,
with the will to do
whatever it takes,
to unshatter
your shattered soul,
to rethink
your unthinkable thoughts,
to eradicate
your fellow-feeling illiteracy.

For,
you've been given the gift
of relearning the language
of civilized dialogue,
to put your brains to work,
improving your chances
to be inscribed
for health of body,
serenity of heart,
radiance of peace,
breath of faith,
and wisdom of mind.

The imminence
of the Heavenly Verdict
brings the lions in our midst,
like frightened kittens,
unabashedly to their knees,
begging the trembling lambs
to forgive their sins.

It persuades the long-suffering
sheep to atone for their failings,
by perceiving all lions
as heartless beasts.

Whatever's the case,
seal us,
O Wisdom and Compassion,
mercifully
in Your Ledger for Life.

# *Simplicity of True Justice*

On this day
 all souls
   lost in the tired clouds—
    perplexed raindrops
    in the mind's
    painted whirlpools—
   will be found
   and
 purified and magnified.

Ascending
 into the day,
  from
   the night
   of
   defeat and humiliation,
  they'll stand fast
 against
any odds.

Wading
 through the hurricanes
  of heavy tears,
   *"heavier than the sands of the seas"*
    under our weary feet,
   we do believe
  it is
the Lord who will
    *"open*
    *the blind eyes,*
   *to bring*
  *out the prisoners*
*from*
 *the dungeon,*
  *and those*
   *who sit*
    *in darkness out*
     *of the prison-house."*
Hallelujah.

O Lord,
 our Compassion,
  strengthen us to reach out
   from the unseen
   mortal vistas of cleverness
  to the inviolable
 simplicity
of true justice.

# *Mutuality of Forgiveness*

Figuratively,
    Yom Kippur
    follows
    the moon.

Yet
    metaphorically
    it outshines the sun,
    hallowing
    a new dawning:
    the magnanimity
    of the divine judgment.

With
    enlightening intensity
    it bestows
    upon us
    a compelling breadth
    of vision,
    to perform
    acts of charity
    in thought and in action,
    to utter
    the right words—
    *repentance*
    and *renewal*—
    at the right time.

Rather
    than allowing us
    to be distracted
    by potential doom
    that may loom
    behind the horizon,
    Yom Kippur places
    in our hands a torch
    amid multiple mirrors,
    reflecting
    a long
    light
    of unweakened
    insight
    and humility in perception
    toward
    the ultimate
    redemption
    through
    the mutuality of forgiveness.

# Soulful Grand Slam

Purifying the mind,
we rededicate ourselves
to the solidarity of the diverse
embedded
in the repenting worlds
that orbit within the divine sparks
of Jewish consciousness.

Yom Kippur
is thus distinguished
from other holidays.
On other holidays we celebrate,
reflect and commemorate.
On the Day of Forgiveness,
we search our souls,
examining our deeds,
breaking our inner devotion
out of spiritual stagnation.

We strengthen the bond
of our brotherhood
with *Klal Yisrael*,
across trillions of rays of love,
helping create
a more humane world
for ourselves, our neighbors,
and future generations.

This is the reason
why the Merciful,
who may forgive
our transgressions against Him,
does not pardon our sins
against one another.
He decreed so,
removing this clause
from His almighty jurisdiction
and making it
our sole responsibility.

There's no alternative,
whether gently blowing
with the breezes of goodness,
or struggling through
the torrents of evil;
chanting a prayer of the heart,
or gracefully gliding with our melodies,
like a singing sparrow in flight;
this is a sacred duty incumbent upon us
to hit again and again
the soulful grand slam,
raising higher than high
our fasting hallelujahs,
from one through all others
unto our Maker's Ears.
Amen.

# Sportsmanship

By harmonizing
    our loyalty
    for one another
    in the perspective
    of perceptions,
    remembrance,
    and tradition,
    we shall play
    the unswayable-by-bias
    team-game
    of truth and liberty,
    mustering strength,
    sustaining
    our fair-minded resolve.

Beyond
    the immediate,
    the unmistakable,
    the readily perceived,
    the apparent and visible,
    we shall continue
    to cope with the most explosive
    exigencies of our day
    in the spirit
    of our inherent sportsmanship.

Looking ahead
    onto the upland tenets
    of life, faith, and liberty,
    we shall reject
    insensitivity
    of divisiveness,
    the dissonance
    of disunion,
    rectifying
    the consequences
    of our self-destructiveness.

We shall weave
    the restructured meaningfulness
    of our destined being
    by synthesizing
    and reuttering
    an ancient prototype
    of our prayers:
    *"May we unite in one fellowship,*
    *with all our hearts."*
    Amen.

# Arpeggios of the New Dawn

There are
    no isolated
    ivory towers any more.
    There never have been.

Being as interlaced
    within complexities
    of our relationship
    with the world
    as we are,
    we know
    that when we are one,
    we can hear
    in the voices of one another
    the sounds of the great *Shofar*
    undaunted by defeat,
    undazzled by triumph.

It's posing now
    the not-enough-asked question,
    "Aren't all of Israel
    brothers and sisters?"

It's Jewishly
    reverberating the answer
    rooted in the anchorage
    of Jewish knowledge:
    the biblical reawakening of joy
    within the miraculous arpeggios
    of the new dawn,
    that carry the *niggun*
    and do care.

Pronouncing
    the most solemn season
    in the cosmic union
    of mesmerizing modernity
    and memorable mysticism,
    we will find
    in one another
    warmth of trust.

We will refresh
    the old dignity
    that comes on this Holy Day,
    raising our beacon of courage
    in theory and in application—
    for you and for me.
    Hallelujah.

# *Hallelujahs*

The shimmering
 blade of grass,
  by
   giving up
    its morning dew
     to rescue
      another's life—
       as though
        resuscitating
         the iridescent soul
          of all the green pastures
           in
            our universe—
            grows
            unto the Lord
            life-affirming
Hallelujahs.

The lonely
 ray of sun,
  by
   turning off
    the glimmer of its eye
     to rekindle
      an extinguished flame—
       as though
        sustaining
         all the stars
          in our
           glittering firmament—
           celebrates
          our homage
         to the infinity
of trust.

The solicitous
 little bird,
  offering
   the scintillation of her voice
    to guide another to safety—
     as though saving
      all the sound of skies,
       commanding to be
        fruitful and multiply—
        fortifies
       in perfect love
      our responsibility,
one for each other.

The humble flower,
 radiant
  with purity,
   sacrificing
    its life-glorifying aroma,
     to succor
      another's
       life-vivifying nectar—
        as though preserving
        all
          the fragrance
           of
             the earth's gardens,
              purifying them
               for
                their yearly inscription
                 in the "Book of Life"—
                recharges
                the power to heal
                and to flourish
                next year in savvy spirituality
and in the perception and lucidity of our well-being.

All
 these thought-stirring praises
  unto the Lord,
   rising from
     their concern for the others,
      establish a mood
       of spiritual polyphony
        glowing with riches
         of quiet warmth,
           perpetuating with inner lights
            the lengthened shadows
             of a newborn symphony,
              ringing with awakening,
               reconciling differences
                in the reverberant
                 interdependence of responsibilities,
                 seeking the instant
                 in the eternity of a smile,
                consecrating
                the poetic marriages
               of the red-and-silvery wild flowers
              with the golden-prairie grass of the sun,
              the yellow-and-pink dreams on the ocean floor
             with the camouflaged scents of hearts
            on the mystery of the Milky Way,
            the lavender lullabies of the spheres
            with the gentle coloraturas of birds' trills.
Hallelujah!

# *Partners for Life*

The most life-giving
of all virtues
resides
in fidelity clasping hands
with loyalty.

It pinpoints
the precept of precepts
that *"Saving a single life
is saving every living thing."*

It is our right,
in times like these,
to probe all the pressures
of our daily problems.

It is our duty
to cope with our daily share
of dilemmas and dramas,
holding each other's hand
with firmness of purpose.

It is our privilege
to nourish the breath of tolerance
within the daily-never-wearied prayer,
walking with the world
as partners for life
in parity of pain
and forgiveness.

As long as we can harbor
the pursuit of Jerusalem,
as the pulmonary vein of our being,
in trust and by promise,
we can synthesize
the eternal templates of self-dignity
and live in peace
through time and tide,
under—and yet nearest to—the sun.

Nothing is more worthy
than rallying
the high-energy humility
of our heritage
into the loftier-than-imagination
standard of living
for the entire human race.

Then,
we will rise,
emboldened like royalty,
ennobled like the poor.
So be it!
Amen.

# Va-Anaḥnu

ואנחנו

*Words: From Aleinu*

*Music: Issachar Miron*

Arthur Szyk

## At the Sukkah

*"Ye shall dwell in booths seven days."*

Leviticus 23:42

# Gate 6
# Sukkot, the Festival of Tabernacles

*Sukkot commemorates from the 15th of Tishri through the 23rd of Tishri (usually October), the period after Exodus, when the Israelites dwelt in the wilderness in "sukkot." It's also celebrated as "The Time of Our Rejoicing" and "Hag ha-Asif."*

Ye shall dwell in booths seven days; all that are home-born in Israel shall dwell in booths; that your generations may know that I made the children of Israel to dwell in booths, when I brought them out of the land of Egypt: I am the Lord your God.

*Leviticus 23:42–43*

On that day will I raise up
The tabernacle of David that is fallen,
And close up the breaches thereof,
And I will raise up his ruins,
And I will build it as in the days of old.

*Amos 9:11*

Just as a man cannot fulfill his obligation on the Feast of Tabernacles unless all Four Species are bound together, so Israel can only be redeemed when all Israelites hold together.

*Yalkut Shimoni 188a*

To the mystic the Sukkah represented the ideal combination of physical and spiritual which is the mosaic of Jewish thought. It is a place where one eats and drinks in an atmosphere of the joy of the festival. It is also the place where one meditates and prays.

*Rabbi Isaac N. Fabricant*, Sukkot
*(Jewish Chronicle Publications, London, 1958)*

May it be Thy will, O my God and God of my fathers, that Thou mayest cause Thy Divine Presence to dwell amongst us, and mayest Thou spread the Tabernacle of Thy peace over us.

*From the Sukkot prayer liturgy*

Gate 6

"Sukkot, the Festival of Tabernacles"

## Gatepost Epigraph

### Spotlighted Shelters

When
gazing through
our sukkot's
branches-with-leaves-open
ceilings
into the loving eyes
of the sunset and the sunrise,
the moon and the stars,
we pray for life-giving rain.

With
the pace of nature,
we remember
the sonorous
symbolism
of the makeshift *sukkot*
as our
spotlighted shelters.

We realize
once again
that nothing
is more fragile
than the stability
of our homes,
as long as not
all our homeless brethren
can dwell
in security
in their shade and light.

From "Communal Possession"

# *Pilgrims at Heart*

Never forget
on this holiday
the fragrant bouquet
of our deliverance
burgeoning in each generation
from bondage to freedom.
Nor fail to ascend
with the poetic purity
of your sensory gladness
to the Jerusalem
of your parents' unanswered prayers.

And here
for the present:
while dwelling
for eight days in *sukkot*,
hone nightly
your binary timbres
of decency and justice
within the motion
of the introspective moon and stars.

Deepened by the hues
of faithful incantations,
celebrate the Holiday,
with the seekers of truth in mind.
Join the pilgrims at heart.
For they're your brothers and sisters.

And that's not all.
Holding hands
with Heaven and Earth,
circle ceremonially
the universal *bimah* of your Jewishness.

Move your subjective processions
around the psychic altars
of your creative-will childhood,
embodied in your soul.
Rise up with and within
the messianic unconscious,
fortifying and forging
your boundless conscious.

Surround with love
your supplications
for the life-giving harvest,
regaling the universe.

Hearten your will
to lead a Jewish life
dedicated
to our ternary quest
for justice, truth, and peace,
residing in your inheritance,
nourished by Israel, taught by the Torah,
and sanctified by the Merciful
(may His holy name be blessed!).

# *Communal Possession*

Blessing the sun,
and rejoicing with the moon,
Sukkot proffers
*etrog* and *lulav*, *hadas* and *aravah*:
the four holiday species.

It embraces Judaically
*"a land of wheat and barley,*
*vines and fig-trees*
*and pomegranates;*
*a land of olive-trees and honey"*—
the seven bounties of *Eretz Yisrael,*
in the savory
spontaneity
of the Lord's signs and miracles
hymning eternity.

When gazing—
through our *sukkot*'s
branches-with-leaves-open ceilings—
into the loving eyes
of the sunset and the sunrise,
the moon and the stars,
we pray for life-giving rain.

With
the pace of nature,
we remember
the sonorous symbolism
of the makeshift *sukkot*
as our spotlighted shelters.

We realize once again
that nothing is more fragile
than the stability
of our homes,
as long as not
all our homeless brethren
can dwell in security
in their shade and light.

Therefore,
we heed the hallowed counsel
of our sages teaching us
that each individual link—
every one of us—is an inseparable part
of our inherited-communal-possession
golden chain: *Klal Yisrael.*

This holiday is then
an open-minded proof
of passion and patience,
verifying that
*"the precepts of the Lord are right*
*and rejoice the heart"*
and that exalted above all
is His broad-minded glory.

# Hineh Mah Tov הנה מה טוב

*Psalm 133:1*                                    *Music: Issachar Miron*

**Deciso, with a dancelike rhythm** (♩=84)

Hi-neh hi - neh mah tov u-mah na-im hi - neh mah tov mah tov u-mah na-im

mah—tov—mah—tov u-mah na-im she-vet a-ḥim— gam— ya-ḥad hi-neh Hi - neh mah tov u-mah na-im hi-

neh mah tov mah tov u-mah na-im mah tov u-mah— na - im mah—tov mah—na - im Chi-bi-ri-

bi-ri-bi-ri-bi-ri-bi-ri - bi-ri-bi-ri-bi-ri-bi-ri - bi-ri-bi-ri-bi-ri-bi-ri-bi-ri bom

Chi - ri-bi-ri-bi-ri-bi-ri-bi-ri-bi-ri bom chi-ri-bom Kol Yis - ra-el a-re-

vim a-re-vim zeh ba-zeh Kol Yis-ra-el— a-re-vim Kol Yis-ra-

el a-re-vim— zeh ba-zeh— Kol Yis-ra-el— a-re-vim— a-re-vim— zeh ba-zeh

Kol Yis-ra-el— a-re-vim a-re-vim zeh— ba-zeh Hi-neh hi-

*Arthur Szyk*

# Simḥat Torah

## Celebrating the Completion of the Reading of the Torah.

# Simḥat Torah, the Rejoicing of the Law

*The last day of Sukkot is celebrated on the 23rd of Tishri (usually October) as "The Rejoicing of the Law." During the festival, the last chapters of the Torah cycle are read. Psalm 118:25 is chanted during each circuit of "Hakkafot"—the joyous processions with the Torah scrolls around the Bimah. In some congregations, "Hakkafot" are made also around the synagogue.*

The God of nature acts alone. The God of covenantal history, however, acts within a relational context. He must weigh His actions, as it were, in the light of how they affect His covenantal partners, in this case, Abraham and his descendants.

*Rabbi David Hartman*, A Living Covenant
*(The Free Press, A Division of Macmillan, Inc., London, 1985)*

Those Jews [of Auschwitz], who on their journey to the end of all hope managed to dance on Simḥat Torah; the Jews who studied pages of the Talmud, without having the books before them, as they carried heavy rocks on their shoulders; the Jews who sang Sabbath songs to themselves as they were being worked to death—they have taught us how a Jew is supposed to behave in time of trouble. For them, the commandment "Rejoice on your festival" was an impossible commandment to observe—but observe it they did.

*Elie Wiesel (1928– )*

An ancient Jewish legend has it that when God spoke at Sinai, revealing the Torah, all Israel was present, the living and the dead and those not yet born, so that every Jew in the course of history has had his personal share of the revelation.

*Lucy Davidowicz*, The Jewish Presence
*(Harcourt Brace Jovanovich, New York, 1960)*

The joy which permeates the Festival of Sukkoth reaches its climax on Simḥat Torah.

*Rabbi Isaac N. Fabricant*, A Guide to Sukkoth
*(Jewish Chronicle Publications, London, 1958)*

EIGHTEEN GATES OF JEWISH HOLIDAYS AND FESTIVALS

## Gate 7

**"Simḥat Torah, the Rejoicing of the Law"**

## *Gatepost Epigraph*

### *Groomed by Our Heritage*

Enlivened
even by a smidgen
of the Simḥat Torah
pristine freshness,
we convey to You
a dreamlike evocation—
a greeting of love
faithborne on wings
of our insight,
dancing to the tune
of the scriptural cantillations
that reecho
wisdom and forbearance.

Revolving
with simple dignity,
in and around
the integrated arrays
of the ethics,
law and liturgy
groomed by our heritage,
Simḥat Torah
is
the world's greatest oxymoron:
the eternal youthfulness
of the age-old glory.
*Happy Holiday.*

From "Youthfulness of the Age-Old Glory"

# *Innovative Cycles*

Is
there anything
new under the sun?
The sun itself
hastens
to affirm its answer.

Its
five million megawatt-hours,
arriving daily
at the doorstep
of our universe,
emanate
uncountable billions
of never-duplicating
hues of light,
painting the skies
with ever-changing nuances
of distinctly different
and newer-than-new
colors of life.

Simultaneously,
the older-than-old
under the sun
grows deeper,
dazzling wiser,
and flowing sweeter
with riches of space,
vastness of oceans,
wondrousness of earth.

The ancient words
with their ever-timely advice,
dancing together arm to arm,
blossom in the unfathomableness of heart,
contemplativeness of mind,
ferocity of lightning,
unpredictability of volcanoes,
measurelessness of simplicity,
destructiveness of earthquakes,
majesty of the kingdom of stars.

On a grander scale
the revival of spirituality
brings
the Mosaic springs and laws
into the reality
of our life,
opening new gates
in the resplendence
of the never-ending
innovative cycles of Torah reading.

Yet,
this holiday
marks more than the rereading
of the chapters
in minutely meshed movement,
like a chronometer's cogwheels
driving each other
year after year,
or as the Torah's *Yad*
oscillating ceremonially
like a time-driven
grandfather's clock's pendulum,
from Simḥat Torah to Simḥat Torah.

Glorifying the Lawgiver
and praying for peace,
this holiday is a testimony,
affirming annually,
that the Lord
inscribed
His blessings on the melted wax
in the interior shelters of our mind,
impressed
His kiss of compassion
upon the lips of our souls,
and struck
his seal of love
on the hearts of iron,
ticking inside our headstrong integrity,
thereupon forging its inner meaning
on, within, and under
the sacred stepping-stones of our tradition.

Enlivened even by a smidgen
of the Simḥat Torah
pristine freshness,
we convey to You
a dreamlike evocation—
a greeting of love
faithborne on wings
of our insight,
dancing to the tune of the scriptural
cantillations that reecho
wisdom and forbearance.

Revolving with simple dignity,
in and around
the integrated arrays
of the ethics, law, and liturgy
groomed by our heritage,
Simḥat Torah
is the world's greatest oxymoron:
the eternal youthfulness of the age-old glory.
*Happy Holiday*.

# Sisu ve-Simḥu   שישו ושמחו

**Hakkafah-Circuits, Simḥat Torah Liturgy**          *Music: Issachar Miron*

Arthur Szyk

# Kindling the Ḥanukkah Lights

*"Blessed art Thou, Lord our God, King of the Universe,
who wrought wonderful deliverances for our fathers
in days of old at this season."*

# Gate 8
# Ḥanukkah, the Festival of Rededication

*An eight-day festival, from the 25th of Kislev (usually December), commemorating the victory of the Maccabees and the purification and reconsecration of the Holy Temple of Jerusalem (165 B.C.E.), the festival is celebrated by the kindling of the Ḥanukkiah, the eight-branched menorah with "shammash" placed in a ninth socket, first lit and then used to kindle the other candles.*

In a thousand years of national existence on the soil of Palestine the Jews over and over drove out oppressors and regained independence, but the Maccabean War, a battle for religious liberty, alone found a place in the rites of our faith.

*Herman Wouk (1915– ), Ḥanukkah Today*
*(from The Hanukkah Anthology by Philip Goodman [The Jewish Publication Society of America, Philadelphia, 1976])*

On the first day of Creation, God imagined light and scattered its rays through time and space. Whenever men turn to Him, in agony or rapture, in humiliation or in victory, His first commandment stands renewed and fulfilled: "Let there be light!"

*Avraham Soltes (1917–1983), Proclaim Liberty—a Ḥanukkah oratorio. (Music by Issachar Miron; libretto by Avraham Soltes. Mcron Music Co., New York, 1967)*

As part of the eternal world-wide struggle for democracy, the struggle of the Maccabees is of eternal world-wide interest.

*Louis Dembitz Brandeis (1856–1941)*

Ḥannukah comprehends Judaism to mean Jewish independence—in the physical and political sense—in that small land on the eastern coast of the Mediterranean where the threefold bond of land, people and faith was forged for all time. . . . On Ḥanukkah we proclaim our confidence that peace will come. It may take time, but it will come. In the measure that Israel's security will be buttressed, her economy broadened and her international status enhanced, the impact of her progress, coupled with peaceful intent, will make its lasting mark on the Arab mind.

*Yaacov Herzog (1921–1972), A People that Dwells Alone*
*(Weidenfeld and Nicolson, London, 1975)*

*EIGHTEEN GATES OF JEWISH HOLIDAYS AND FESTIVALS*

### Gate 8

**"Ḥanukkah, the Festival of Rededication"**

## Gatepost Epigraph

### Effervescent Push

If
the Holiday morals
solemnize
with concision
and clarity
the recurring factor
of our trust
in freedom
for all,
then the Ḥanukkah message
of rededication
gives us today
an effervescent push
to go on, sing on,
and
pass on
its spiritual light,
from
parents
to
children,
and
children's children.

From "Eight Candles"

# *Recipe*

Unlike
the ubiquitous pancakes,
they're not some
trifling nibble.

Their royal,
obligatorily audible crispiness
is of Hasmonean ancestry—
secure
among
the greatest
in the epochal
pantheon of crustiness.

When
we peel
their
proud paterfamilias,
the potatoes,
we separate
the peripheral
from
the essential.

When
we grate them,
fashioning their new image,
we safeguard
their nutritional
sacrosanct substance,
regenerating
the strength
of crunchiness,
the puréed treasure trove
of golden batter,
and the relativity of weight
as the concrete metaphors
of faith
consuming might,
in culinary terms.

When
we mix the ingredients,
whisking in spices,
stirring in eggs,
and
frying the mixture,
we see
that by absorbing
discrete elements,
we come out
enriched and ennobled.

Anything that would give
perennially so much,
deserves more
than just a thank-you.
But they don't need our gratitude.

Just savor their
predictable freshness
and epistemological aroma,
scenting with sensible sophistication
the frying pans of freedom.

At this juncture,
having whetted our convictions,
judiciously,
gastronomically,
and spiritually,
it's time to examine
both sides of the hot issues,
enjoying the cuisine of the free.

And now, let us relish
the deep-fry resonance
of the earthly
and the heavenly,
abundantly providing
for the stomach-deep reconciliation
of an ancient recipe with new horizons.

Henceforth,
prompted by the occasion's breadth,
we're eager to tickle
the conspicuous softheartedness
of mouth-watering delectability
and the fire-tempered endurance
of an iron skillet.

Of all things, *latkes*?
. . . and why not?  What?!

On matters of taste, a prejudiced opinion
should never rule in my kitchen.

By now you should know—
they're phenomenally real, of epic proportions,
and . . . (with both hands on the fork)
flavorsome and prayerful.

They—the *latkes*—are the healing charm of taste,
tickling in four harmonic cadences
the spiritual palates
of light, dedication, nobility, and thanksgiving.
So? . . . Bon Appetit, and Happy Ḥanukkah!

# *Kaleidoscope of Faith*

On wings of breathtaking harmonies
    of faith and glory,
    we
    celebrate
    with polyphonies of pluralism,
    the victories
    of
    spirit over might.

We offer Him
    our thanksgivings
    for
    starting
    His magnum opus
    with
    light.

We are
    the luminous
    tone color
    of
    the *Symphonie Fantastique* sonorities
    for
    repeated obbligato meditation.

Since nothing, seemingly,
    can follow
    our celebration
    except anticlimax,
    we
    close
    our
    universal
    spectacle of light each year
    after the eight nights' run,
    but we remain
    faithfully Yours.
    Forever.

We are
    Ḥanukkah's nine-candled mirrors—
    authentic kaleidoscopes
    of universality and faith,
    viewed
    from each separate angle of perception.

# Anatomy of a Jew

It's an agile top
　　with a four-sided body
　　　　firmly based on a single point,
　　　　　　unable to balance itself
　　　　　　　　unless accelerated into fast motion.

When whirling,
　　its dramatic flair implies
　　　　that to flourish,
　　　　　　freedom must always
　　　　　　　　be bold, diverse, and kinetic.

Every now and then,
　　even when entering difficult times,
　　　　it dazzles with the ancient alacrity
　　　　　　of potent energy
　　　　　　　　and balanced power.

In matters of fairness—
　　fiercely combative—
　　　　it habitually disguises itself
　　　　　　as weakness
　　　　　　　　(and is not).

It is a thoroughly modern
　　affirmation of faith,
　　　　which does not need to be reaffirmed being always there!
　　　　　　(And yet, as a pattern of life, for our own sanity,
　　　　　　　　it's reaffirmed three times daily, anyhow.)

And, behind its mystique,
　　what happens when
　　　　it stumbles on a stone
　　　　　　in its path
　　　　　　　　tumbling to the ground?

Does it imply defeat?
　　What kind of a question is that?
　　　　It isn't easy. This can happen to anyone.
　　　　　　But . . . the answer is:
　　　　　　　　"not at all!"

Under persecution's very nose,
　　in bold defiance of pain, sorrow, doubt, and death,
　　　　the side on the bottom manifests a sweeping proclamation
　　　　　　of self-rebirth and self-reformation
　　　　　　　　in its ways of justice, compassion, and peace.

Bursting
　　with fresh oxygenous love of liberty,
　　　　it aerobically emphasizes
　　　　　　that the biblical reality of hope is unfathomable
　　　　　　　　and that its melody spurs an even faster movement.

And so, whether it's grappling
　　or tripling its twirling,
　　　　it's always bouncing back with grit
　　　　　　onto the heights in quest of moral responsibility.

Outnumbered everywhere,
   it spins out
      iridescent youthfulness,
         rekindling in your heart—
            an unending festival of lights.

Despite contradictory rumors,
   it is an unstoppable
      dedication of a free soul,
         calling for the redemption
            of the prophetic spirit.

It's a creative vanguard,
   defying science
      and gravity, and generating
         the perpetually oscillating bond
            from one heart to another.

Closing the distance between
   past and present, it is a cheerful
      exponent of respect for every living thing,
         with an abundance of spirituality
            for the whole of humanity.

Now. Take heart and just think
   of its promise,
      galvanizing integrity and grandeur,
         for it is: the dream of the dreidel
            swirling up in a Ḥanukkah smile.

Does this *"Dream of the Dreidel"* guess
   jolt you into awareness? Well. Probably,
      but only into what's on the surface.
         It's just a hand-holding hint.
           And that's all.

So, to the point,
   what is it?
      Is it our soft-spoken human touch
         moving swiftly in circles
            as a purling spectacle?

Is it our autobiography
   rapidly changing
      reflections from different angles
         in the kaleidoscopic pattern
            of our history?

May be,
   but what is indiscernible
      to your naked eye,
         your heart can see it with clarity,
           and you know it.

And yet, more than anything else,
   in the inwardness
      of our feelings,
         it is an ethical enigma of a believer.
            Yes. It's the anatomy of a Jew.

If
might
is
concrete,
even when
walking
the longest and the shakiest tightrope of your life;
and spirit
stays
tenaciously abstract,
even
when
head
down
on
a flying trapeze;
then
the victory
of spirit
over earthbound might
affirms
the reconciliation
of the absolute
within
humanity's infinity of faith.

If
your dream
is
still as though dwelling
thousands of miles
high up
in the stratospheres of daring,
then,
if you're
not afraid
to grapple
with
precedents proving that
"this can't be done!"
remember,
your heavenward quest
for bringing it
into
living reality
is
just
right here,
in the summits of your will.

# *Eight Candles*

EIGHTEEN GATES BY ISSACHAR MIRON / GATE EIGHT: HANUKKAH / EIGHT CANDLES

If
    the myocardium
    reigns
    aerobically
    muscular
    when
    riding unconsciously
    between the cars
    of
    imagination;
    and
    the conscious
    solidity of space
    becomes
    invisible,
    even
    to
    some intellectual minds
    with
    acuteness of vision;
    then
    miraculously
    the universality
    of these eight candles
    still illuminates
        our shadowed pathways of today.

If
    the Holiday morals
    solemnize
    with concision and clarity
    the recurring factor
    of our trust in freedom
    for all,
    then the Ḥanukkah message of rededication
    gives us today
    an effervescent push
    to go on, sing on,
    and
    pass on
    its spiritual light,
    from
    parents
    to
    children,
    and
        children's children.

# *Velocity*

Its
millennial light
brings
the eight-night affirmation
of the ascending trajectory
into eternity.
It
is
never dimmed
and
never diminished,
though it kindles
the billions
of
my heart's sensors.

It enriches
all the self-reliant stars
of my heritage's solar systems
with the velocity of faith and courage
without ever being impoverished.

Is it
an extraterrestrial reflection?
An echo
from a far-off constellation?

Quite diametrically opposite!
How human it is.
The same roots,
the same cosmos,
the same historic necessity
of life and freedom.

Tracking the targets of indifference,
it's the same splendor
of continuity
and the same
vigorous and full-bodied
challenge for renewal.

And
if
it's so,
light up
your face
with
a smile.
It's Ḥanukkah!

# *Prayer*

May

the Festival of Light,
commemorating
the great
miracle
that
happened there,
shine
and
bless you here.

May

it bestow
upon you
health,
good friends,
and
peace of mind.

May

it bring back
to
the threshold
of
our troubled generation
the mutuality
of
compassion
and
understanding
among fellow people.

May

it harbinger
an era
of
happiness
and
warmth,
fulfilling
the universal visions
of peace
through freedom
for the survival
of Maccabean values
to light
all those still-dark alleys
of humanity.

# *Nocturnal Octet*

Being a blessing,
    a nocturnal octet
    of
    hope,
    this Ḥanukkah
    is
    a celebration
    in the unison
    of faith and freedom.

O Heavenly Father
    of
    all peoples,
    give us strength
    and wisdom
    to
    transcend
    the boundaries
    of
    prejudice
    and
    ignorance
    with
    civility of discourse,
    with
    equanimity to differ,
    and
    with a live-and-let-live attitude.

O Father of compassion,
    bless us
    with
    wisdom and courage,
    compassion in mind,
    and
    charity of heart.

O *Avinu Malkeinu*,
    grant us
    a telescope of generosity
    to see the light of tolerance
    through the darkness of the day
    and a megaphone
    of brotherly love
    to proclaim to the world
    our message
    painted blue and white
    over
    the heavenly spectrum of all colors.

*"Watchman,*
*what*
*of*
*the night?"*
*The watchman*
*said:*
*'The morning*
*cometh*
*and*
*also the night.' "*

Although
still
surrounded
by
the pervasive mutability
of
the descending darkness,
let's welcome
the persuasive vitality
of
morning's ascending light:
It
cometh along!

May
it
restore
our predilection
for
Maccabean miracles,
as
a daring adventure
in
a dream
come true.

May
it make
the horrors
of
yesterday
into
a potent source of energy,
rekindling our courage
and clinching yet unrooted hope
to dwell inviolately
in our hearts.

# *Biblical Beams*

Born
    of the breath
    of biblical beams,
    our fantastic voyage
    into
    real life's eternity
    bewails
    the vulnerability
    of heroes,
    symbolizes
    the invincibility
    of martyrs,
    and restates
    the indivisibility at heart
    of the torn apart—
    on-line
        and off-line.

And
    here's how:
    It pours forth
    memories
    eternizing
    the fragrance
    of cut flowers,
    evoking
    the depth
        of perception.

In harmony
    with
    the universe,
    it celebrates
    the multicellular equity
    of spirit,
    unraveling
    the ABCs
    of fair play,
    and *italicizing*
    the relativity
    of joy and anguish
    in defeat
        and victory alike.

# *Proof of Permanence*

It studies
the wholeness
of the broken hearts,
discovering
the pragmatism
of hope as the mainstay
of sanity,
raising spirits
within our quest for light.

The holiday
re-creates every day
the miracle of miracles
in the short-lived
beauty of a butterfly
as a visual-image
proof of permanence.

To fathom
the unfathomed
depth of truth,
to fortify the entireness
of the dispersed,
to hearten
the invincibility
of fair play,
to immortalize
the life of the cut flowers,
the holiday
keeps alive our dream
interned in the gulags of Jewish suffering.

Restarting its autumnal tradition
of filling stumbled hearts
with courage—
consciously or subconsciously—
Ḥanukkah keeps
for us on the maps
of the mind
the riches of freedom,
building the body
and steeling the soul.

# *Courage of Compromise*

Our
middle-of-the-road morality
counsels us to be *"pliant as a reed"* and . . .
apparently even in our self-interest,
not to be *"hard as cedar"*—
which spotlights for us anew
the mightiest of all talmudic weapons:
power of understatement
and courage of compromise.

So,
we remain unbiasedly unafraid
to appear
as the most
high-powered "weak"
on earth.

Yet,
in times when Jewish lives
are threatened again,
when the Vatican's
generations-late-in-arriving
*Nostra Aetate*
had not prevented
snakes of bigotry
from globally raising
their treacherous heads,
when terrifying thresholds of fire,
poison gas, and deadly missiles
must be crossed again and again,
Ḥanukkah biblically rekindles
for us that little spark
of the Maccabean spirit
that dwells inside our collective breast.

It makes us
chafed at the rednecked notion
stereotyping the Jew as victim,
forging us to defy it
by impelling us
to keep an unblinking eye
on bias from any source and any direction,
to hold the line boldly
and be strong,
sustaining without fear or malice
inside every Jewish heart
the untempered-by-guilt lesson
of the few with farseeing faith
on how to prevail
over the many
with shortsighted might.

# *Light Is Oneness*

Why
is it
that
the *menorah*
of
Ḥanukkah
is eight-branched,
and not seven-branched,
like
the Holy Temple's indestructible one
carved into Titus's Arch,
now with the rebirth of Israel
spiritually repatriated
to rejuvenate its eternal flame
in Jerusalem?

Doesn't
the seven-branched *menorah*
kindle in each generation
the seven flames
of our tradition:
love,
freedom,
justice,
charity,
pioneering spirit,
faith,
and learning?

The Ḥanukkah *menorah*
has these seven
branches
reinforced
by one more.
And why?

Because
the eighth branch
is
an injunction
to remember
that darkness
is
disunity,
and
never to forget
that light
is oneness.

Amen.

# Ḥanukkah Portals

Even
    if it's true
    that
    my orbiting brain
    commands
    more connectors
    than the combined
    telephone networks
    throughout
    our universe;
    and even
    if it could be proven
    that my own retina
    contains hundreds of millions
    more light-detecting cells
    than
    a commuting combustible comet,
    still it is certain
    that the earthly
    miracle of miracles
    in faith and science
    retains
    the allegorical luminosity
    and the gravitational
    radiation force
    of my tiny and fragile,
        eight multicolored candles.

On a more personal level
    in the here and now,
    their wide-eyed vision,
    traveling
    aloft on its fiery chariots—
    reappears, with its sparkle of wonder,
    on my subliminal portals
    more frequently than their constellatory kin,
    not every seventy-six years
    like the dazzling Halley,
    but cyclically
    as my millennial light,
    dependably—year by year—
    touching
    with its flaming fingertips
    the *mezuzah* affixed
    to the right-hand
        doorpost of my soul.

# *Engrossing Epitome*

Despite
the horrors
of the Holocaust,
Ḥanukkah
affirms annually
the soundness
of my reliance
upon
the engrossing epitome
of Jewish lore.

It unifies
religion with reason,
divine supremacy
with earthly democracy,
and
adherence to every law
of *Shulḥan Aruḥ*.

Yet it bestows
the gift
of prophetic freedoms
upon everyone
to codify
an
intimately moral
code of life
in accordance
with
one's own conscience
that's
consummately cushioned,
since
the Patriarchs—
by
the Providential Protection:
blessed be He
at any time
and
at any hour.

# *Oasis*

If there's a holiday
   for
   renewal,
   this is
     the one.

Yet,
   as
   in a life policy,
   it
   assures
   a lower value
   on renewal.
     Why, why?

Isn't it clear?
   To
   keep pace
   with this trend,
   it
   impels us
   to
   give more of ourselves,
   to
   work harder,
   to
   weave our dreams bolder,
   to
   deepen
   our personal
   *"Ani Ma'amin"*
   and
   to increase
   our dedication
   to the morality
   and
     ethics of our parents.

Then let the aura of Ḥanukkah
   renew the flame
   of our aspirations,
   fire our imagination,
   and flow with joy
   and happiness
   as a life-giving stream
   in the oasis
   of our
     desert dreams.

# B'raḥot Ḥanukkah    ברכות חנוכה

*Ḥanukkah Liturgy*      *Music: Issachar Miron*

DEBORAH

*Arthur Szyk*

## The Prophetess Deborah
**Holding Court Under a Palm Tree.**

# Gate 9
# Tu bi-Shevat, the New Year for Trees

*Tu bi-Shevat is celebrated on the 15th of Shevat (usually January or February). It's also the anniversary of the inauguration of the Knesset (February 14, 1949) in Jerusalem.*

For there is hope of a tree, if it be cut down, that it will sprout again, and that the tender branch thereof will not cease.

*Job 14:7*

O Thou, who first planted trees eastward in Eden, and hast created on earth a resemblance to Paradise through the overarching beauty of leaf and branch—we thank Thee for the gift of fruit and shade, of food and shelter, which Thy Divine wisdom has provided for the children of men. To our forefathers, wandering through the wilderness of Sinai, the sight of a tree meant respite from from the beating rays of the sun, an oasis of refreshment amid the devouring desolation of the desert.

*Avraham Soltes*, Invocation: A Sheaf of Prayers
*(Bloch Publishing Company, New York, 1959)*

In the mountain of the height of Israel will I plant it; and it shall bring forth boughs, and bear fruit, and be a stately cedar; and under it shall dwell all fowl of every wing, in the shadow of the branches thereof shall they dwell.

*Ezekiel 17:23*

A weary wayfarer through a desert came at last upon a tiny oasis, where a mighty tree grew near a spring. He sat down in the shade of its luxuriant branches, ate of its luscious fruit, drank of the clear water, and rested and refreshed himself. When he was ready to depart, he said to the tree: Wherewith can I bless you, seeing that you are already blessed with beauty and shade, with magnificent branches and delicious fruit, with a precious location and a spring for your roots? Let me then wish you that all your offshoots be like you!

*Talmud, Ta'anit*

## Gate 9

### "Tu bi-Shevat, the New Year for Trees"

## Gatepost Epigraph

### Earthly Biblical Continuity

Now,
rooting
a thriving sapling,
as an ecologically heartfelt
welcome
of the living soil
for
every new immigrant
arriving to Israel,
it bespeaks
a kindly heart
of the earthly biblical
continuity.

In that way
Tu bi-Shevat
redecorates
each season
a different facet
of the divine beauty
from
the garden of Eden
for us here
on land
and
as a picturesque Hallelujah
for the heavens.

From "Interdependence"

# Growing with the Trees

Its
lineage
goes back
into
the morning
of the third day
of
creation
when the Lord made every tree
grow out of the earth.

It
epitomizes
a state of dramatic flux,
renewal, affirmation,
beauty,
and
continuity.

It has as many roots,
firmly clasping each other
deep inside the earth,
as it has lofty branches in the sky,
like our heritage,
reaching out above,
higher than high
and freer than free.

When broken,
it expands,
sprouting budding shoots
with pained determination
and vigor.

All its life it keeps
growing and germinating
new and novel ideas,
prefacing, anticipating,
initiating and reigning
for another year.

It
has weathered all storms
and withstood raging fires.
Just like our very being,
it represents
a renascent life,
a season of marking time,
in the cycle of growing with the trees.

It's
impossible
not to be struck
by
their aromatic richness,
bite-size integrity,
nutritional versatility,
and
palatable poetry
engendered
by
the gardens
of
creation.

The New Year of Trees,
robust
and
self-reliant
as
its
trees,
is
here
complementing
contrapuntally
each
newborn infant
with
a newly planted tree.

It's
again on the way
to life,
with
life
beyond
the bounds
of
time,
of
space,
and
our tidal state of mind.

It is
the primordial urge
of
rootedness and growth.
It's  Tu bi-Shevat.

# *Interdependence*

The biblical
>granddaddy
>of
>all New Years
>for
>trees
>in orchards,
>groves, and forests
>is spanning
>the globe
>and theatricalizing
>nature's riffs,
>rhythm, and phrasing
>within
>the human interdependence
>>with trees.

Purifying air
>with a suave touch
>of life-giving oxygen,
>draining swamps
>with
>inconspicuous energy
>and turning them
>into
>orchards
>ripe with fruit,
>it paints
>the once-unalterable desert—
>>green—into livable soil.

Muting noise,
>vocalizing
>in tranquillity
>with motion
>of branches and leaves,
>it is foresting
>mountains,
>guarding bountiful
>farmland—everywhere—
>versifying
>embryonic valleys,
>halting
>in its real-life tread
>>earth's erosion.

We're
>> refreshed
>> on Tu bi-Shevat
>> by the gentle
>> fruit-fragrant
>> breezes
>> serenading
>> unto the Lord
>> canticles of miracles,
>> poetizing
>> with olives,
>> dates,
>> and figs,
>> rhyming
>> with pomegranates,
>> carobs,
>> dancing with raisins
>>> and almonds.

Proffering
>> shade
>> to the tired,
>> it reincarnates
>> recreational
>> retreats
>> for children
>>> of all ages.

Now, rooting a thriving sapling,
>> as an ecologically heartfelt welcome
>> of the living soil
>> for every new immigrant
>> arriving to Israel,
>> it bespeaks a kindly heart
>>> of the earthly biblical continuity.

In that way
>> Tu bi-Shevat redecorates each season
>> a different facet
>> of the divine beauty
>> from the garden of Eden
>> for us here on land
>> and as a picturesque Hallelujah
>>> for the heavens.

# Ha-Zorim be-Dimah   הזורעים בדמעה

*Psalm 126:5*     *Music: Issachar Miron*

**Brightly, and spirited (♩=120)**

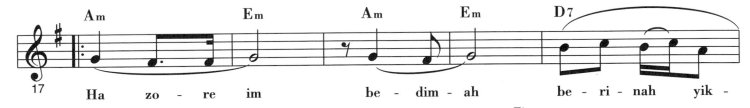

## Second Letter of Purim

*"Then Queen Esther, Daugher of Aviḥail, and Mordeḥai
the Jew, wrote with full authority to ratify this second
letter of Purim.  Dispatches were sent to all the Jews, to the hundred and
twenty-seven provinces of the kingdom
of Ahasuerus—with words of peace and truth."*

# Gate 10
# Purim, Feast of Lots

*Purim is a day of joy and thanksgiving observed on 14th of Adar (February-March) in commemoration of the miraculous deliverance of Jews in ancient Persia as chronicled in Megillat Esther (the Scroll of Esther).*

Consequently, these days should be remembered and celebrated by every single generation, family, province, and city; and these days of Purim should never cease among the Jews, nor shall their remembrance perish from their descendants.

*Esther 9:28*

We celebrate Purim, but without singing the Hallel, because we are celebrating a reprieve from death in a world where murderous evil forces continue to be a threat.

*Rabbi David Hartman*, A Living Covenant
*(The Free Press, A Division of Macmillan, Inc., New York, 1985)*

And they all ordained with a common decree in no wise to let this day pass undistinguished, but to mark with honour the thirteenth day of the twelfth month (it is called Adar in the Syrian tongue), the day before the day of Mordeḥai.

*2 Maccabees 15*

Mordeḥai left the King's presence clad in royal apparel of blue and white with a large gold crown and a robe of fine linen and purple; then the city of Shushan was cheerful and glad. The Jews had light and gladness, and joy and honor.

*Esther 8:15-16*
(The Megillah: A New Translation *by Rabbi Meir Zlotowitz, Mesorah Publications, Ltd., Brooklyn, 1976)*

Mordeḥai's intention was to unify all Jews throughout the world in the celebration—even those Jews who had tried to escape Haman's decree by fleeing, and who, therefore, thought their own personal safety had not been jeopardized. *(D'na Pashra)*

*Rabbi Nosson Scherman*, The Megillah
*(Mesorah Publications, Ltd., Brooklyn, 1976)*

EIGHTEEN GATES OF JEWISH HOLIDAYS AND FESTIVALS

## Gate 10

### "Purim, Feast of Lots"

# Gatepost Epigraph

### Envoy Extraordinary

Deflating theatrics,
the scroll
tells us that Purim
is not only some
hurly-burly leaps of history,
self-deprecating joyful stunts
with hyperactive rhythms,
kaleidoscopic effects,
parades,
pranks,
floats,
foolery,
carnivals filled to the brim
with rapid-fire frivolity,
all amusingly
interwoven with tradition.

In fact,
and to a greater degree,
Purim
is an envoy extraordinary
of relief,
comforting
through laughter.
It's a tender tune
to cheer up.
It's a spellbound sight
for sore eyes.
It's a tongue-in-cheek
stronghold
buttoned up against evil
of cosmic reach
and earthly grip.
And in retrospect,
it's a spark spectrum
of common destiny uniting Jews.

From "Tongue-in-Cheek"

EIGHTEEN GATES BY ISSACHAR MIRON / GATE TEN: PURIM / ENVOY EXTRAORDINARY

# *Who Am I?*

It's a time for rejoicing.
 So today, if anything,
 I show off and exult,
 poeticizing an exuberant festivity,
 joking, boasting,
 eating, drinking,
 rollicking
 and clowning
 and, for that reason,
 making of myself
 the laughingstock
 of our megafun jubilation
 to gladden your heart.

For the moment,
 I am the affirmative-action merrymaking testimony
 to the oldest antibigotry,
 antisegregation civil rights struggle,
 in a sprightly (yet untritely) manner
 chocked with chuckles.
 (It's just the way I've been born.  I can't help it.)

Right from the start, I retell
 the enigmatically mythical
 *Megillah* chronicle,
 laying out in circular form
 an ancient tale:
 of wrath,
 political intrigue,
 piety and grand love,
 handwoven
 like an Oriental rug
 with dazzling threads of history.

Meanwhile my psychoanalytic loom—
 textured by the interlocked
 weft and warp threads,
 knot by knot, row by row—
 illuminates
 up and down, left and right
 an operettalike rapid-parlando narrative.

It focuses on four central characters:
 *Ahasuerus*—an aging Persian king,
 his teenaged Jewish wife—*Queen Esther*,
 *Mordeḥai*, her pious cousin and political advisor,
 and the royal vizier—*Haman*, a haughty deputy
 plotting to destroy
 the entire Jewish population
 in 127 provinces of the empire,
 from Samarkand to Kush.

Mounting fanfares
       beneath the busy beehives
       of drumbeats and noisemaking,
       I stomp feet, whirl flags
       rattling the youthful *greggers*
       (in the old layered style).

I sing and cry firing salvos of humility
       loaded into the grooves
       of laser discs, thanksgiving for the miraculous
       deliverance of our brothers and sisters.

The logic for my position, and in a way of my very being, is
       that I enlighten your eyes to comprehend,
       your minds to perceive, your hearts to feel,
       adding your voice of a prayerful petition
       to an open-and-shut day of introspection and faith.

It is ironic that though I've been
       so often accused by my detractors
       of having been fickle and frivolous,
       in fact, I remain in the webs of life's vulnerability
       the serious, sincere, and loyal zest for living.

What am I jolly for?
       Just take a deep breath.
       Lean back, just a bit . . . in memory.
       Unstiffen your upper lip . . . of history.
       Follow your nose . . . to discovery.
       Then lifting up your eyes onto your life's promontory,
       look straight into mine for your own line of ancestry.

After a while, cup your ear and listen:
       I am the yardstick of the bygone teardrops.
       I am the search for your spiritual fortitude
       in proximity, distance, and infinitude.

In short, by now, I suppose
       you should know what I really am:
       In the Jewish historical context,
       I am a defensive smile mightier than might,
       longing for liberty that's dwelling inside your heart.

So finally, may I now draw the line?  What's the issue? ! ! !
       Would I lie to you?
       Am I not all at the same time:
       agony and ecstasy,
       force and farce, faith and fun?

Then when you're awash in bliss,
       feeling  freedom in each of  your bones—that's me.
       And that's why I want you to know,
       that whether high-in-the-sky,
       or inexorably down-to-earth,
       when my solitude masquerades as bursts of hilarity,
       my gallows humor acts freakishly,
       and my mind is overwhelmed by playfulness,
       like a needle in a haystack is by hay . . . that's me.
       For I am Purim!

# Tongue-in-Cheek

The *Megillah*,
a salient story holding
the adult and teenaged audience rapt,
makes young girls scream
and little boys
skip like wild goats.

It concludes
most un-Jewishly with . . .
a Hollywood world of fantasy-like
moving-picture solemnity,
revving up a romantic,
state-of-the-art happy ending,
accelerating
an exuberant-climactic sequel,
and tummling at a screwball party lasting
one hundred eighty pompous days and nights.

Its morale fire-breathes magic,
bringing you the injunction to stand
on the little square
of your Mosaic principle,
never to despair, when biblically
confined helpless in the belly
of a contemporary whale,
not to lose all hope
when drowning
in the seas of hopelessness,
and not to lose heart
when compelled by Hamans to wear
gas masks in sealed rooms
or even when allowed
by Ahasuerus' obese passivity
to be shoved under the turf
into harrowing darkness.

Deflating theatrics,
the scroll tells us that Purim
is not only some hurly-burly leaps
of history,
self-deprecating joyful stunts
with hyperactive rhythms,
kaleidoscopic effects,
parades, pranks, floats, foolery,
carnivals filled to the brim
with rapid-fire frivolity,
all amusingly interwoven with tradition.

In fact, and to a greater degree,
Purim is an envoy extraordinary of relief,
comforting through laughter.
It's a tender tune to cheer up.
It's a spellbound sight for sore eyes.
It's a tongue-in-cheek stronghold
buttoned up against evil
of cosmic reach and earthly grip.
And in retrospect, it's a spark spectrum
of common destiny uniting Jews.

111

# *Downplayed Pain*

Domestically,
 I am the uproarious propensity
 galloping
 through the ever-changing tonality
 of the vulnerable
  twists and turns.

I am
 the dancelike perception
 of perpetual persistence,
 rocking around the clock
 and covering my downplayed pain
 with the zaniness of oompah accompaniment
 and the farce of image-pursued rhythms
 of sociable whimsicality,
 fretting brilliance like the mischievous waters
  over the stones in a brook.

I am generosity to the needy,
 gentle genial gifts and gaiety for loved ones.
 I am thriving in agile songs,
 tossing off endless coloratura ripples
  racing upward with ludicrous playfulness, ever higher . . .

I am the boisterous buffoonery
 shaking the blues
 in the tummling scales of an integrated,
 worldly-wise jubilation celebrating
 not the demise of a global outlaw—Haman
 on the very gallows he erected—in an evil scheme—for the Jew,
 but the affirmation of ordinary Jewish values,
 put into action by Mordechai with skillful simplicity,
 the pleasingly girlish posture
 of Queen Esther's responsible righteousness,
 the victory of the unassuming, downtrodden folks,
 who—standing on the edge of oblivion—had the moral strength
 to lead, all the time, their threatened lives—in perfect faith—
 even under the shadow of their
  then imminent genocidal massacre.

And now,
 blot out your memory of Amalek—whirling noisemakers,
 drink *le-ḥayim* with zest
 (yes, today it's not only permitted but enjoined),
 say a prayer of thanksgiving
 for the Purim miraculous deliverance,
 and laugh with your Hallelujahs.
  (It's not only judiciously required but providentially welcomed.)

112

# *Purim Pâtisserie*

Our fame got spread by word of mouth.
We are the three-cornered sweet pastry,
nicknamed after Haman—*Hamantashen,*
reflecting history's fickle vicissitudes for good and evil.
(We accept this affront defyingly and yet . . . yummily.)

Though we're habitually humble,
can't we rightfully boast
of our chewy-voluptuous-bittersweet bellies
filled cravingly, in a crunchy crescendo,
with queenly mouth-watering goodies of the classiest mien
to gratify your gastric senses grindingly
and to be out-and-out secreted in your mouth?

We're the culinary adventure
of the sonorous goodness,
a gourmet-gallant guide
to the epicurean pleasures inside
and their sensuous treasures outside,
flying onto the fortissimo climaxes
of having the audiovideo-flavorful fun
to tickle palpably your fastidious palate
with speed and directness to exhilarate and stimulate.

Whenever the whole world quivers—
like a hungry, fear-struck jackrabbit—
feeling so low that it wants to scream,
just remember
that our savory-honeysweet friendliness
( . . . though, unbearably bitter for bigots)
will always stay with you in taste and in truth,
as a faithful rapid-fire shot of deliciousness
sprucing irresistibly your soul
and as a tour de force for your sweet tooth.

Making our one-dish cuisine plain, we'll keep
our open prune-jam-and-poppy-seeds eyes on you,
spanning for you a fresh-doughy-safety blanket
of the nourishing Purim pâtisserie—
an aromatic triumph of grandma's quality,
opulently fit for a king, lavishly delicate for a queen,
spasmodically chirping sotto voce—
not like a bunch of gossipy crickets out by the barn,
but gliding molto cantabile in roaring cascades of salivation
down through the esophagus into the snug confines
of the sanctum sanctorum of your cheering stomach.
And if so, isn't now the time for a healthy holiday hiccup?
Hearty appetite to you:  So, *be-te'avon* of the toppest echelon!

Arthur Szyk

# Reading the Scroll of Esther

*"Blessed art Thou, Lord our God, King of the universe,
who has sanctified us with His commandments
and ordained that we read the Scroll of Esther."*

# Gan Ḥayot shel Purim    גן חיות של פורים

*Words: Anda Amir*        *Music: Issachar Miron*

Scherzando, mischievous, with humor (♩=152)

Kol ha-re-ḥov hu gan ḥa-yot ar-na-vot va-a-ra-yot

par-pa-rim u-fi-lim du-bo-nim ve-a-ya-lim

Ein pa-nim be-lo ma-se-ḥah Pu-rim kol ha-ir se-me-ḥah, Pu-rim!

Ne-me-rim ve-ki-po-dim a-na-kim ve-ga-ma-dim

ze-ke-nim vi-la-dim ya-ḥad ya-ḥad me-rak-dim

Ein pa-nim be-lo—— ma-se-ḥah Pu-rim kol ha-ir se-me-ḥah, Pu-rim!

Va-a-fi-lu ha-ya-re-aḥ ba-sha-ma-yim shat sa-me-aḥ

ma-se-ḥat a-na-nim me-ḥa-sah lo ha-pa-nim

Ein pa-nim be-lo ma-se-ḥah Pu-rim kol ha-ir se-me-ḥah, Pu-rim!

*Arthur Szyk*

## Around the Family Seder Table

*"We were once the slaves of Pharaoh in Egypt,
but the Lord our God brought us out from there
with a mighty hand and an outstretched arm."*

*The Passover Haggadah*

# Gate 11
# Pesaḥ, the Festival of Freedom

*A festival commemorating from the 15th of Nisan (usually April) the Exodus from Egypt, Pesaḥ is observed for seven days in Israel and for eight days in the Diaspora.*

At the birth of Jewish history, our people left Egypt and marched to Mount Sinai for the most momentous rendezvous in history—the morning when they saw the Revelation and heard the Ten Commandments.

*Rabbi Nosson Scherman*, Art Scroll Machzor
*(Mesorah Publications, Ltd., Brooklyn, 1984)*

Have you read the "Song of Songs" of King Solomon? Well, read it again and you will find it all that I could tell you. . . .

*Heinrich Heine (1797–1856)*
*(Lewis Browne*, That Man Heine, *Macmillan Co., New York, 1927)*

You shall not oppress a stranger, for you know the feelings of the stranger, having yourselves been strangers in the Land of Egypt.

*Exodus 23:9*

Passover represents not only remembrance of deep scars and memories of past persecution. It is no coincidence that Passover is to be celebrated in the spring; for it also is meant to carry a message of hope and anticipation.

*Theodore Bikel (1924–)*
*(Mark Podwal*, Let My People Go: A Haggadah
*[Darien House, New York, 1972])*

From the day the Israelites left Egypt and fashioned into a people out of a mass of slaves, they shared common memories and hopes.

*Philip Birnbaum*, The Birnbaum Haggadah
*(Hebrew Publishing Co., New York, 1953)*

# EIGHTEEN GATES OF JEWISH HOLIDAYS AND FESTIVALS

Gate 11

**"Pesah, the Festival of Freedom"**

# Gatepost Epigraph

### At His Word

Bursting

into song,

it brings back

to the fore

the sacred writ

prophesying

that

"none shall make us afraid"

and exhorting

the world,

it's high time

it woke up,

got out

of its troubled bed,

seized

the moment,

and took the Bible

at His word.

**From "None Shall Make Us Afraid"**

# *Wheels of Passover*

Passover
is
a hidden expressway
of
wheels within wheels,
sounding
never-failing hope
in
each generation.

On
their axles
rotates freedom;
every hub
is
a lifeline
of
tradition;
the spokes
reverberate
love
and
compassion.

The "re-spring-ing"
of
Jewish spirit
revolves
endlessly new
horizons
around
their rims . . .

and
the whole
vernal complex
of
wheels within wheels
is
rolling on
as a holiday
of youthful faith—
turning
inward and outward,
backward and forward
in history—
spinning in time
as
the intrepid awakener
of our unity.

If it's a holiday
    for believers,
        it's a commemoration
            of a struggle,
            for those
            who keep
            the torch
            of freedom aflame.

If it's a time of mourning
    for those who grieve
    the oppression
    of our people,
        it's a warning to watch out
            for Pharaohs
            of today.

If it's a family reunion
    for the scattered,
        it's a multicourse feast
            for the
            discriminating,
            four cups of wine
            for the epicure,
            the excitement
             of anticipated
            gifts for children.

If it's a singsong festival
    for music lovers,
    four questions
    for the discerning mind,
        it's all these
            and many
            more
            things
            for many others.

In an era of global
    chaos and impatience,
        it's an epitome of springtime,
            a cornucopia of dreams
            stopped short of pretentiousness,
            bestowing
            upon you and me
            the self-awareness of today,
            the understanding of yesterday,
            and the range of seeing for tomorrow.

So have fun. It's Passover.

# *Aptitude for Liberty*

Being a victim
    of ignorance,
abused
    by bigots,
oppressed
    by tyrants,
downgraded
    by narrow dogmas,
rejected
    by neighbors,
betrayed
    by friends,
tormented
    by all shades
    of inhumanity,
discriminated against
    by whole societies
    to whose well-being
    he valiantly
    contributed,
    the Jew delved deeper
    into the meaning
    of freedom
    in his world
    of perpetual pain and prejudice.

This
    developed in us
    an aptitude for liberty
    and a fortitude
    in meeting
    hardship and danger.

In each generation,
    its attainment
    for ourselves,
    and in behalf of our
    brothers and sisters,
    white and black,
    gives birth
    to martyrs and heroes
    of the great cause,
    often forgotten by history,
    yet lovingly molded
    by rays of Israel's sunshine
    into the golden chain
    of our heritage.

# Burdens of Love

The Jew nourished
    Passover—in place and in time—
    saw it growing and becoming
    (even on the edge of the abyss)
    burdens of love,
    labors of dedication,
    and harbinging the Law-Giving then and now.

And he cultivated it
    as the hub of family togetherness,
    the nerve center for mutual support,
    a prelude of justice
    to the season of universal freedom
    in an ambience of personal fulfillment,
    friendship, and peace of mind.

In that way
    Passover has evolved
    as a blessing of blessings,
    a well-remembered source
    of eternal truth
    within the acuteness of its spirituality.

It gives definite expression
    to intuitive revelation
    of biblical visions
    and modern dreams.

It sounds a unifying chord
    in the ascending harmony
    colored with a nuance of Jewish mysticism:
    *"Next year in Jerusalem."*

Maturing,
    it continues—cosmically—
    to be forged on the storm-beaten
    mountain peaks.

It's a sign of hope,
    melodizing with the heavenly waterfalls,
    canoeing through the life-giving rivers,
    walking with us hand in hand on earth
    across the sunny valleys of inner strength.

It tenders re-creation and rejuvenation
    in the shadowed pinewoods of salvation
    for all humanity.  Everywhere!
    Amen.

# *Wish*

May this Passover
be a passing over
the darkness of dejection,
rising to the high noon of light,
invigorating our pursuit of peace.

May it be a messenger
bringing to our shores
the good tidings
of springtime
whistling a multivoice round
with Elijah's whirlwinds.

May it resound with laughter
of gratification
in our eternal trial and error,
soul-searching
our temperamental hope.

May it reach out
toward the path
of our unflappable resolve,
rejuvenating
the vernal quest for renewal.

By His grace,
may its national epic
restore the common voice
of self-understanding,
healing the miracle
of self-redemption
in our collective memory.

May it rouse the sunrise
in our inner psyche,
bringing back
to our pained generation
the vibrancy of fellow-feeling.

May it link with responsibility
each one of us to another,
fostering inwardly new trust
and advancing outwardly
the love of mankind,
without which life
cannot survive on this planet.

# *Passover Prayer*

May
this Passover prayer
come true:
that you
and
your loved ones
*"go your way . . .*
*with a merry heart,"*
with
courage of conviction,
with
broad-based integrity,
with
faith in our future,
with
individuality and perception
in
our conscientious scenario
for
sane human relations
and
caring
one for the other,
always
and forever.
Together.

*"Hear,*
*O ye heavens,*
*and*
*give ear,*
*O earth,"*
unity is
not a burden!

The holiday
is a moral asset,
a light,
a bond
of strength.

It is up to us
to keep our step
in tune
with its spirit.
It's what
we need most.

*Mo'adim le-Simḥah!*

# *Color-Blind Polyphony*

The *Haggadah*
focuses
on the past
but
is an evocation
of
the present,
implying the primacy
of
recounting
and
reviewing:
recounting the struggles
of
a flight from
bondage to freedom,
and
reviewing
what we should be doing
to keep this
most
precious treasure
of liberty
alive.

Passover
is then
a color-blind but color-enthralled
polyphony of freedom,
strengthening
the hearts
of the free
and
of those still in
slavery's chains,
thus
heralding the world over
that
revolt against
oppression
is
a supreme command
always sanctified,
always obligatory
for humanity's sake
and
for our own.

# *Holographic Lighthouse*

The Holiday of Redemption
calls us this season
to reaffirm spiritually,
inside
the wilderness
of our day,
the vitality
of our deeds
toward
the free-flowing currents
of our commitment
to our heritage,
accessible
only by ferries of faith.

It challenges
the waterfalls
of mankind's complacency
by reawakening
our inborn rapids
of equality,
edging around the cliff
from bondage toward freedom.

It ignites
in each generation
the blessed flame
wrapped in courage,
and spreading light
like a holographic lighthouse
to be viewed
from many different angles,
over
the seas, beaches, islands,
deserts, fields, rivers,
hamlets, and big cities
of our down-to-street consciousness
here, there, and everywhere.

Happy Passover.

# *None Shall Make Us Afraid*

Passover
    is our annual update
    impelling us to hold steadfast
    to our purpose and actions,
    restrenghtening us to sail on
    against the storms
    stirred in each generation
    by the ominous reincarnations
    of pharaohs, ferdinands, isabellas,
        hamans, hitlers, and husseins of the day.

Its  perpetuation
    of Exodus's legacy—
    living as the motivational mandate
    within ourselves—
    transcends its springtime sense of romance
    by inspiring us:
    to stay committed
    on our passage to freedom,
    to part the modern Red Seas
    in self-defense,
    to plunge with faith
    into the threatening waters,
    to leap over
    the pounding nightmares of memory,
    to advance
    between the two tidal walls
    of oscillating waves—
    but, when they're tumbling waterily down to drown—
    it coaches us
    in the the most rapid of all strokes
    on how to surge upward,
        breaking the surface toward a new dawn.

Bursting into song,
    it brings back to the fore
    the sacred writ prophesying
    that "none shall make us afraid"
    and exhorting the world,
    it's high time it woke up,
    got out of its troubled bed,
    seized the moment,
        and took the Bible at His word.

# Giant Among Dwarfs

Exciting
imagination
with
mystery,
impenetrable to scrutiny,
expanding
humanity's horizons
lunarly beyond
the *one giant step*,
remains
the millennial
riddle of riddles,
a giant among dwarfs,
juxtaposing
spurts of miracles
with
disarming simplicity.

Surpassing
the impressiveness
of its pyramid-building contemporaries,
the festive once-in-a-springtime balladeer
continues
to sing in my own backyard,
keeping the balance
of our universe:
the crumbliness of matter,
the temporariness of might,
as against the invincibility
of prayer.

So, while
ten million stars in the sky
are being snuffed
out every 24 hours,
our springtime visitor
endures and radiates
more sparkling energy and light
than the sun's trillions of tons of nuclear fuel.

Its bells ring out
a pristine proclamation, announcing that
the Passover idea of freedom,
like pure art, is absolute
and alive forever in the heart of the believer.

# *Prophetic Miracles*

Like
>
> the parting waters
> of the Red Sea
> that set free the oppressed,
> our own personal *exodus*
> liberates us—the perplexed,
> out of those locked
> closets of our brain
> into the open galactic
> spaces of our mind,
> while the conglomerations
> of stars sipping the four cups
> sing the horizontal-onward-eight-days'
> > hallelujah sonorities.

Deciphering
>
> hieroglyphics
> concealed by millennia,
> below the spiritual sea level,
> deep inside the spring-cleaning
> stations of human spirit,
> the Exodus
> conjures up prophetic miracles
> rejuvenating the forming
> of the Jewish people
> as a nation
> > on the same foothold as all the others.

It's commanding us
>
> to remember daily
> that freedom
> has to be earned
> every waking moment,
> > so long as we live.

Its ever-living moral
>
> reestablishes our energy,
> generating wavelengths
> with the predilection
> for transcendence,
> affording the comprehension
> of elucidative light
> to the essentiality
> of defensible frontiers
> > for liberty and equality.

It restores in each generation
>
> impartiality of justice
> as the royal diadem
> in the hand of our heritage
> and in our own realization
> of its vitality
> as the nucleus of our being.
> > Just like air.  Just like air.

# *Passover Power*

Now as then,
because our *Redeemer*
has kept us alive
and maintained us,
the good-hearted
Holiday of Springtime
has arrived.

It casts
a luxuriant sunbeam
on today's dream
of a saner tomorrow,
with *Elijah*
looking over its shoulder,
and sending us
pink and ivory harmonics
that are real, warm,
and exquisitely earthly,
quickening on each
of his *Seder* nights' visits
(through countless centuries),
the process
of Jewish revitalization,
tonight, in Israel's rebirth,
strengthening
the purity
of its spirit
and value for life on earth.

Seeing
the prophecies
from the Bible
becoming
a modern-day reality
in perpetual bloom,
we stand up to be counted.

By reflecting
our sages' attitude
that a celebration of life,
like study,
is a venerated form of worship,
we add more
power to Passover,
making
its light from Sinai shine again!

# *Redemption's Esperanto*

Evoking
    universal challenge,
    igniting
    the spirit
    with
    purity and beauty,
    the Holiday stages
    a multimedia dramatization
    animating
    a multi-image repudiation
of despair.

It
    looks
    into the eye of our faith,
    nursing
    the renewal of trust
    in ourselves,
    in humanity,
    and in the Book
    as
    a poetic,
    educational masterpiece
    and
    as the absolute
    literary-religious credo
    for all seeking fulfillment
    in this season
of rejuvenated faith.

Pondering life's
    splendors and pitfalls,
    listening
    to our hearts' dictates
    of conscience,
    this pilgrimage
    to the spiritual roots
    of our being
strikes inward.

Passover explores
    the apocalyptic perspectives
    within those revolving circuits
    of flight and rescue
    as the closest thing
    to redemption's *Esperanto*,
    breaking
    through the thickest walls,
    climbing over the highest fences.
    It is engineering
    its own renaissance in hope
for all.

I still wonder
why none
of the ultramodern
high technology
has managed to unearth
the architectonic wonders
(I *built for Pharaoh store-cities*
*Pithom and Raamses*)
or, for that matter,
the remnants of the Covenant tablets.

To the nearsighted,
I am too distant,
for the sophisticated,
too dated.
In the motion-picture industry
I am
Cecil B. De Mille's *Ten Commandments*.
In literature I am a fiction.
In archeology—
on earth and on seabed terrains
and in cosmology—
among the millions of stars
of the Milky Way,
I remain
a mosaic of biblical motifs
nowhere to be found.

Isn't it then clear that
I am an annual rehearsal
of my people's
collective memory,
mirroring their visions
and forging their belief
in the unconquerable
cohesion of solidarity?

Am I not
a *tête-à-tête* with eternity,
standing
with each generation
at the frontier of tomorrow's
world every day?

132

# *Microdisks of Memory*

I am imbued
with the morals
impressed
within the enveloping murals
of psychology as the distinction
between image and mandate,
legitimacy and symbol,
Mount Everest and Mount Sinai.

For I am the
world's record-holder
entrenched
within the democratic soul-searching quest,
throughout the forty-year-long,
psychotherapeutic self-sustaining hardship
videotaped in the wilderness,
inside
the rainbowy swirl of my mind.

In spite
of this lot of issues,
real and imaginary
(each of which,
like a piece of a puzzle,
is revealing piecemeal a detail,
rather
than unfolding the entire picture),
I am the oral history
loaded
for posterity
into the high-density
microdisks of memory.

As from time immemorial,
attesting
to the powerlessness
of power when
employed
by the wickedness of bigotry,
and the invincibility
of unarmed faith,
I am
the night-and-day divine graffiti
sparkling on the wall
of a believer's bulletproof heart.

# *Common Language*

The holiday is a study
in the common language
of ideals and ideas
spanning time
and
an unaffected twilight hour
of self-identity contemplations,
transcending
the course of my own saga.
I am nondoctrinaire
humility in action—
listening, learning, and loving.

It's
the swelling blaze
of that inextinguishable flame
atop the Holy Mountain
testifying
against
the ecclesiastical stakes
of the Inquisition
that precipitated
centuries of pogroms
and the unimaginable
chimneys of the Holocaust.

Passover—
the embodiment of freedom—
is still anguished
by the mass-gassing death vans of Chełmno,
still horrified
by the Holy See's Concordat with Hitler,
a corollary of the convents
that harbored Nazi perpetrators
of crimes against humanity.

Its spirit remains
still suspended
in the air,
hovering
over
the innermost heart's battlefields
of every day.

Its struggle and sacrifice
still reside
within
the inseparable realms
of life, equality, and freedom.

# Dispatch

I think
I am a civilized instinct
of the brotherhood of man
and
a keeper of the misery,
joy, and warmheartedness
of the ordinary, decent
*kleine menschelech*,
rediscovering
the fair-minded spark
of Samsonian helplessness,
in their tacit teardrops
and in the inaudible cry for help
of their laughter.

I
am the poise and plasticity
of Emma Lazarus's palette,
painting
the *"masses yearning to breathe free"*
with
the glorious simplicity
of
all and equal colors.

In short,
belying
the *Nineteen Eighty-Four*
hypotheses
of
the potential omnipotence
of tyranny,
far beyond
the sociological glory
of
the four cups of gladness
and
the psychosomatic effect
of the homebound
bitter herbs' symbolism,
I remain,
your faithful friend—
the invisible but omnipresent—
Passover dispatch.
Free in the lands of the free!

# *Quantum Leap*

Long before
the quantum leap theory,
it revealed
the relativity
of might
versus
the cosmic absoluteness
of my conscience,
second to none
in
its cognitive gravity
on
the solar planets
of my body and soul.

Far more
than fleeing
Pharaonic bondage,
it embarked
on
its space-time-and-motion
epoch-making voyage
to the self-willed sanity,
moral perceptions,
and
poetic sensibility
in
the firmament
of
my heart and mind.

Beyond
mysticism
and sublimity,
it presaged that,
despite the daily risks,
I fear
the complacency
of slavery
rather more than
its genocidal travails,
or
even my state
of aloneness,
being abandoned
in my agony
by the world.

# *Continuum of Challenge*

Passover sustains
a cyclic
continuum
of
challenge,
promulgating
an unchallengeable legacy:
to
cherish,
as
the most honey-flowing
of
all divine mysteries,
the prime-time awakening
of
belief in ourselves
and
in our brothers and sisters.

In
the covenantal transcendence
of Exodus morals,
it weaves
its primal magic
through the miracles
of
freedom,
fairness,
family warmth,
and friendship,
flowing
like
mighty rivers
into
the dawns of eternity.

Breathing
broad-mindedness
for all,
it
imbues all
engulfed
by flames of oppression
with
the perennial potency
of hope reborn
to be free.

# *Answer*

Is there a reason
why
the Passover drama
repeats itself
year
after
year?
I wonder. . . .

But
there is
an answer,
the same
as that given
by our
fathers and mothers
to
their oppressors
in
each generation.

Even though
the entire world
is waging war
against us,
we continue
to seek peace.

Even though
the oceans
of hatred threaten
to drown our people,
we continue
to love.

Even though
we're dispersed
all over the world,
we continue
to be one.

Yes, the answer
is the same;
and it will always
be the same:
we are one.

# *Clothes of Liberty*

When the violets burst
    through the melting snow into their
    reddish-white-and-blue blossom,
    the spring bulbs of our credo
    begin to bloom endearingly
    in our conviction,
    conveying that though
    some of our brothers and sisters
    still remain in chains,
    we must affirm every day
    the lesson of Exodus
    and its message
        of hope for today.

It is contingent,
    now as in those days
    in the wilderness,
    on our willingness—
    and, if need be, any sacrifice—
    to vivify the new
        soul of freedom in each generation.

We know that when breathing
    the healthy way,
    as equals in peace and love,
    and wearing
    the clothes of liberty,
    we can make the entire world
    a better place to live in,
    for our sake and for the sake
    of all those
    who, because of prejudice
    and ignorance,
        hate themselves by hating us.

So, when seeing
    the light of the sun
    gliding like a whistle
    through the lowering clouds,
    let's make this Passover
    again the purposeful heartland
    of liberation,
    ready-made for sing-alongs
    about slavery
    turning into full-bodied independence,
    ringing with music and verse,
    redolent like flowers
    from the Song of Songs' orchards,
    and telling the world about
    the vernal force
    of the prayed-for redemption.
        May it come soon in our day!

# Elijah's Cup

Why does Elijah's cup embody the everlasting hope for freedom?      Is it because Passover regenerates and reunites two diametrically opposed extremes, the empirical and the visionary? Does the Holiday separate the holy from the profane, accentuating and inno-vating the substantive matters of our daily life?  Does it mo-tivate us in each generation to aspire indomitably toward the attainment of the triply basic egalitarian aims of life: freedom to live politically, economically, and socially as equals among equals, or to welcome, as a notion of a simple faith, the annual visit of the ever-living Prophet, heralding peace and messianic redemption?      Thus, Elijah's cup, roaring like a waterfall, brimming with bliss, opens the doors of our homes to mighty rivers of inner energy, resilience,  and self-respect, forging vernal currents of self-fulfillment, and emboldening our *"zeal for the Lord, the God of Hosts."*

EIGHTEEN GATES BY ISSACHAR MIRON / GATE ELEVEN:  PESAH / ELIJAH'S CUP

# Mayim Rabim

מים רבים

*Song of Songs 8:7; 1:7*

*Music: Issachar Miron*

**Warmly, flowing as a joyful stream ( ♩=128)**

141

## Warsaw 1939—Fighting the Nazis

*"We shall not say that we have walked the final road,*
*though iron skies will still bow down their iron load,*
*our longed-for day, our hour will finally arrive,*
*our endless-thousand throats will shout —We are alive!"*

*"Zog Nit Kaymol," by Hirsch Glick, translated by David M. Miller*

# Gate 12
# Yom ha-Sho'ah, the Holocaust Day

*Yom ha-Sho'ah, the Memorial Day to the six million Jews who perished during the Holocaust, is commemorated on the 27th of Nisan in accordance with a resolution passed by the Knesset on April 12, 1951, proclaiming it as "the Holocaust and Ghetto Uprising Remembrance Day—a day of perpetual remembrance for the House of Israel." The Chief Rabbinate of Israel suggested that relatives of the heroes and martyrs of the Holocaust whose date of death remains unknown say Kaddish in their memory on the 10th of Tevet (the Fast of Asarah be-Tevet), decreeing it as the "Day of Kaddish."*

When the Nazis went after the Jews, I was not a Jew, so I did not react. When they persecuted the Catholics, I was not a Catholic, so I did not move. When they went after the workers, I was not a worker, so I did not stand up. When they went after the Protestant clergy, I moved, I reacted, I stood up, but by then it was too late.

> *Martin Niemöller (1892–1984), German Lutheran clergyman*

Not all victims were Jews, but all Jews were victims.

> *Elie Wiesel (1925–)*

A thousand years will pass and the guilt of Germany will not be erased.

> *Hans Michael Frank (1900–1946), governor general of occupied Poland, before he was hanged at Nuremberg on Oct. 16, 1946*

To resist the dehumanizing, brutalizing force of evil, to refuse to be abased to the level of animals, to live through the torment, to outlive the tormentors, these too were resistance.

> *Martin Gilbert,* The Holocaust
> *(Holt, Rinehart & Winston, New York, 1985)*

As the Hebrew poet Bialik once wrote, not even the devil himself could dream up an adequate revenge for the death of a single child. . . .

> *Golda Meir (1898–1978)*

EIGHTEEN GATES OF JEWISH HOLIDAYS AND FESTIVALS

Gate 12

"Yom ha-Sho'ah, the Holocaust Day"

## Gatepost Epigraph

### The Last of the Last Witnesses

As

long

as the heart

of our universe

keeps pumping life,

forlorn and despairing

as we are,

we—the weeping willows,

the last

of the last witnesses—

we will adhere

to our vow

to remember

in thundering quiet,

uttering

Your

Holy Name.

From "Kaddish of Whys"

# *Kaddish of Whys*

On this saddest of days,
        we cry like children in the dark,
        crossing the Valley of the Shadow,
        like blameless leaves
        blown off pilotless
        before their given earthly tenure,
        term and time from the tree of life.

We, the offspring
        of Your servant Israel,
        beg You,
        O Master of Compassion,
        to comprehend in divine terms
        the magnitude of the human suffering
        inflicted upon the best of us—the six million
        of Your homeless, defamed, degraded,
        burned, and buried-alive children.

Tremblingly we question Your passivity,
        which the world regarded
        as Your indifference to our agony,
        and what seemed to many of us
        as Your unilateral breach
        of the never-to-be-severed sacred bond
        eternally binding You, O Lord,
        and Your covenantal partners:
        Abraham and us—his descendants,
        in those cataclysmic years of war
        between the forces of good
        and the devil's minions
        that brought upon us
        the hell of naked bestiality
        no evilest human could ever conceive
        would exist on the sand-blind earth
        and beneath the deafened sky.

We ask:  How could a human mind comprehend
        that Your heavenly eyes, opened omnipotently
                to their utmost eternal expansion,
            couldn't see the enormity of wickedness?
        How could so many nations become accomplices
        to inexplicable cruelty by averting eyes, turning away
            and standing unaffected with impunity on the soil
        soaked seven knees deep with the blood of the innocent?
        How could they pretend not to see, not wanting to know,
    watching the genocide and not condemning the diabolic crime?
        How could so many remain closemouthed, grimly self-centered,
                triggering catastrophic collisions—contemptibly inert
Tarquemada's inquisitors disguised as sheep in their pitiless indifference?
How could so many fail to aid even the very few who could have been saved?

145

On this day
> when the shivering pastures
> still shed tears with their morning dew,
> bowing before You
> we submit our petition
> that You, *Avinu Malkeinu*,
> summon the divine Court-on-High,
> to investigate
> why this calamity happened,
> calling and cross-examining witnesses,
> interrogating the perpetrators
> of this most monstrous of crimes
> against heaven and earth,
> and presenting its findings
> for Your judgment,
> as a providential primer, an eternal random access memory
> and a precedent for the courts of history,
> O our Father and King.

On this day
> of terrible truth revealed,
> when reciting Psalms with our palms clenched,
> every atom monitoring
> the integrated circuits of our subconscious
> is filled with the forged strength of lost illusions
> within the barbed-wire solitude of our being.

As long as the heart of our universe
> keeps pumping life,
> forlorn and despairing as we are,
> we—the weeping willows, the last of the last witnesses—
> we will adhere to our vow
> to remember in thundering quiet,
> uttering Your Holy Name.

Yet, through each one
> of the proverbial seventy-thousand miles
> of our walk of life,
> standing on tiptoes we will lift high up
> to the windows of heaven
> the ever-burning and never-consumed
> question mark of our loudest lamentation
> that survives only in the memory of our people.
> Why, O Father, did Your mercies fail You?

On this day of pain,
> we're still birched with twigs of virulent hate,
> and our eyes are reddened in anguish.
> On our hunched shoulders
> we carry humbly uphill
> our never-failing faith,
> bearing the buckets full of heavy sorrow,
> still too terrifying to be believed.

Haunted by nightmares
      of tormenting memories
      beating their way like crows
      from one aching heart to another,
      we bend down with trepidation
      to see our inner reflections
      in the outer, dehumanized
      oceans of heartlessness, veiling hell upon earth:
      the beloved and the pure—
      the two million Jewish children
      savagely torn from the bosoms of their mothers
      and hurled like coal into fiery furnaces—
      we beg to know:  why didn't You rescue them
      with miracles and wonders
      from drowning in poisonous floods?

In this world and beyond it,
      deep inside our shattered hearts
      handing over to our children the testimony of horrors
      that defy human credulity,
      we the perpetually perplexed
      ask You to listen to the heartbeat of our supplication
      within the wilderness of our spirit,
      and to tell us:  why have You forsaken us?

On this day,
      enduring the unendurable,
      choking in our minds on smoke
      from the *Final Solution* crematoria,
      still nauseous in our hearts from the venom
      of the *Wannsee Protokoll*, we keep as a warning,
      on the optical scanners of our psyche—the memory
      of its scorpion's stingers—eager to whip, to jab, and to kill.

In the saintly footsteps
      of your servant Levi Yitzḥak ben Sarah of Berdichev—
      clinging to the cliffs of the indecipherable
      and praying the unprayable, as he did—
      we won't budge, even one step,
      for Your Silence cries out to us louder
      than all our planet's mightiest megabels.

O Father, Your Silence
      is blowing the electromagnetic fields
      of our brain, yet it's not erasing
      even a single memory byte of our martyrdom.

Bearing the unbearable,
      out of the wholeness of our broken dreams,
      we the carriers of loyalty of endless generations to You
      raise our shrouded voices and ask You again
      to accept, O Father, our Kaddish of Whys:
      *"Yitgadal ve'yitkadash Sh'mey Raba"*
      and answer us, O Lord:  wherefore?
      And why?
      Why? . . .

# Dawns of Renewal

In the desolated
galaxies of our mind,
we never forget
Chagall's floating visions
of crucified Jews,
who in their helplessness
prevailed
over their tormentors
and the abysmal indifference
of the world.

On wings
of perplexed memories,
barbed-wire fences,
and chimneys
of mankind's inhumanity,
we juxtapose today—
as every day—
the cognitive upheavals
of abomination and hatred
with dawns of renewal
overwhelming the darkness.

Our hearts
still pulse with pain,
breathing sparks of life
into the growing crescendos
of Abraham-Isaac
dreams and destinies
to improve the earth
for Thine own sake.

Twining
the courage of resistance
with the unsung triumphs
of defenselessness,
we refresh
the streams
of inner strength
woven into fugues
of suffering and glory.

May
our firmness of faith
evoke
compassion and passion,
heartening us
in the ongoing war
between good and evil.
Amen.

# *Honest Handshake*

We are
    the seven-branched heart,
    always on the beat
    with the celestial melody
    of Your reborn promise
    to Israel,
    O Master over Life and Death.

Despite
    the Holocaust,
    we shall always
    remain
    the ever-timely
    manifesto of courage,
    reaffirming
    around the clock of our life,
    the honest handshake
    with You, O Father,
    on Mount Ararat's harbors
    for the endless generations
    of the Flood's survivors,
    and on the Sinaitic altitudes
    of human faith,
    replctc
    with eclectic accents
    and transcendental vitality.

Now,
    when taking charge
    of our own destiny,
    ours is
    freedom of choice.

Ours is willingness
    to make a new start
    a mode
    of egalitarian evocation,
    redeeming
    the eternal masterwork.

And ours is new hope,
    reawakening
    the phoenix of humanity's conscience,
    on whose suffering,
    rebirth,
    and promise
    the youthfulness
    of Your and our universe depends.

# Ḥalom va-Zemer הלום וזמר

*Words: Hayim Hefer*      *Music: Issachar Miron*

**Moderato, with tenderness, and long flowing lines (♩ =92)**

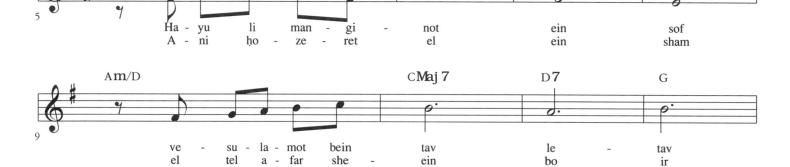

Ha - yu li man - gi - not    ein    sof
A - ni ḥo - ze - ret el    ein    sham

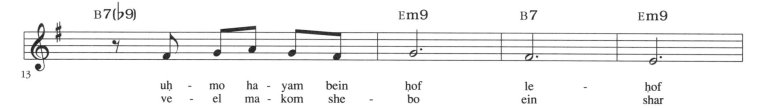

ve - su - la - mot bein   tav    le - tav
el tel a - far she - ein    bo    ir

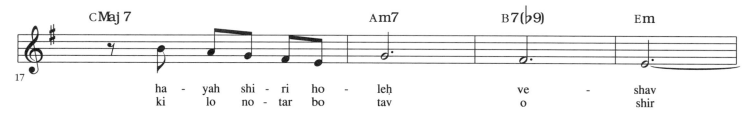

uḥ - mo ha - yam bein ḥof    le - ḥof
ve - el ma - kom she - bo    ein    shar

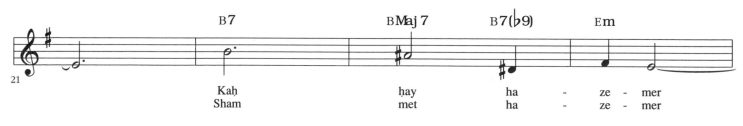

ha - yah shi - ri ho - leḥ    ve - shav
ki lo no - tar bo tav    o    shir

Kaḥ    ḥay    ha - ze - mer
Sham    met    ha - ze - mer

el ko - ḥa - vim hu him - ri
rak ha - ḥa - lom a - hu - vi

151

*Arthur Szyk*

## Israel's Independence Day Scroll
*"Justice, justice shalt thou follow, that thou mayest live,
and inherit the land which the Lord thy God giveth thee."*

*Deuteronomy 16:20*

# Gate 13
# Yom ha-Atzma'ut, Israel Independence Day

*Yom ha-Atzma'ut is celebrated on the 5th of Iyyar (coinciding with April or May), commemorating the promulgation of Israel's independence (May 14, 1948). When it falls on a Sabbath or on a Friday, it is celebrated on the preceding Thursday, in order that it not desecrate the sanctity of the Sabbath. Yom ha-Zikkaron, the "Remembrance Day" for the defenders of Israel who fell during its War of Independence and subsequently, precedes Yom ha-Atzma'ut and is observed on the 4th of Iyyar.*

On this Israel Independence Day, we can see the vision of the prophets fulfilled before our very eyes—the restoration of *Zion* and the ingathering of our people from their dispersion.

*Shlomo Goren (1917– ), Chief Rabbi of the State of Israel*
*(Israel Independence Day Haggadah, United Jewish Appeal,*
*New York, 1976)*

On our festive day, let us review in joy and thanksgiving the mighty deeds of the past and let us resolve to apply ourselves with all our might and all our hearts to the new efforts of the future.

*David Ben-Gurion (1886–1973)*

What would Israel do, what would Israel be without Diaspora? Yet the fact remains: the Jewish people, dispersed as it is, does not live in a state of siege, while you, in Israel, have made your homes on the front lines; your children, not ours, confront perils every day; you, their parents, not we, enter anguish every night.

*Elie Wiesel (1928– ), A Jew Today*
*(Random House, New York, 1978)*

I am not a fair weather friend who says that I support You [Israel] only as long as I can bask in Your reflected glory.

*Paul Jeser, CLAL's Newsletter (1988)*

I the Lord have called thee in righteousness, and have taken hold of thy hand, and kept thee, and set thee for a covenant of the people, for a light to the nations.

Isaiah 42:6

# Eighteen Gates of Jewish Holidays and Festivals

Gate 13

"Yom ha-Atzma'ut, Israel Independence Day"

## Gatepost Epigraph

### The Pangs of Its Coming

Even
when betrayed,
You
transform
one uncertain day
after another
into
an era
of trust
and belief in Yourself
and the world.

Yet,
You're still
so vulnerable
in Your
invincibility.
You've come
a long way,
but
the  redemption
as foretold
by the prophets
isn't here yet,
still writhing
in the pangs
of its coming;
but
come it will—
reliantly—
like the planets
moving
about the sun.

From "Rose of Israel"

You're
linked
to the magnetic chains
of our universe,
making us
responsible
one for another,
like metal-borne electrons,
protons,
and neutrons,
orbiting in and around
the spiritual nucleus
of our being.

Without
You,
our civilization
would have disintegrated
as if devoid of metals,
our tradition
would have collapsed,
lacking
Your galvanizing power.

If
You're hammered
anywhere,
we
resound
as beaten brass
among the hills,
everywhere.

In the main,
You're
densely solid as iron,
of
high lustre as gold,
and
strong as titanium.

If
You're scattered
to pieces
like mercury,
we
all disperse,
only to regroup
and
reunite
in one indivisible whole.

In spite
of Your
every-day-to-be-remembered-
and-never-to-be-forgotten
agglomeration
of anguish,
in spite
of Your countless wars
for survival,
in spite
of *intifada*
and Scud missiles,
You
radiate
the zest for life
stronger than ever,
brightening
our pathways,
generating
a grand design,
and reflecting
the evolving typefaces
on Your storyboard.

Your
vitality
and vision
keep
the world's eyes
blazing,
the adrenaline
of moral values
pumping,
accelerating
the affirmation of faith.

Even
when betrayed,
You
transform
one uncertain day
after another
into
an era
of trust
and belief
in Yourself and the world.

Yet,
You're still
so vulnerable
in Your
invincibility.
You've come
a long way,
but
the redemption
as foretold
by the prophets
isn't here yet,
still writhing
in the pangs
of its coming;
but
come it will—
reliantly—
like the planets
moving about the sun.


Three times
a day we pray:
May it
come soon
rolling down
as the thunder
from the heights,
calibrating
by the clock
of the older
than old
and the newer
than new,
reconciling
the reality
and the dream,
and blessing You
to bloom
and be strong
all the days of Your life,
O Rose of Israel.

You've
        been turned
        to ashes—
                countless times.

Multitudes
        of Your children
        have been blown out
        like a blaze of light,
        cut in their bloom
        before they could lift
        their rising song unto the hills
        to help sustain earth's life-giving orbits
                around the sun.

Alas,
        through the ages,
        Your temples,
        schools, dwellings were put ablaze,
        and You were unabatedly abused
                and abased.

And yet . . .
        each time You've risen
        from Ezekiel's Valley of Dry Bones,
        stemming the tide,
        bringing
        Your best blossoms forward,
        reinvigorating
        Your breath of courage,
        beaming
        Your inextinguishable spark
        of inner dignity for Yourself,
                for Your friends and for Your foes—alike!

You're still so young
        and yet,
        Your children include:
        the patriarchs and matriarchs of the Bible;
        Moses "whom the Lord knew face to face";
        the judges of old;
        the Sweet Psalmist of Israel;
        Solomon, "in whom was the wisdom of God, to do justice";
        the prophets of the Lord;
        the loving and beloved women of valor,
                Miriam, Deborah, Ruth, and Esther.

Your Jewish morality candles still illuminate
        the pluralistic windows of the world,
        with schools of Hillel and of Shammai,
        with Saadia Gaon, with David Ben Zakkai,
        with Maimonides, with Spinoza, and with Nachman of Bratzlav,
        with Gaon of Vilna, and with Ba'al Shemtov,
        with Heine, with Proust, and with Freud,
        with Bergson, with Buber, and with Einstein,
        with Sholom Aleichem, with Pasternak, and with Tuvim,
            with Kafka, with Agnon, and with Wiesel.

You're the paragon of the Jewish soul,
        still ringing out of Zion the beauty
        of Mendelssohn, of Mahler, of Ravel,
        of Offenbach, of Meyerbeer, of Milhaud,
        of Gershwin, of Bernstein, and of Copland,
        of Wieniawski, of Heifetz, and of Piatigorsky,
        of Schnabel, of Horowitz, and of Rubinstein,
        of Bernhardt, of Muni, of Jolson, and of Kaye,
        of Pissarro, of Modigliani, of Epstein and of Chagall,
            of Cardozo, of Brandeis, and of Frankfurter.

You're the growing tree of life
        of the Jewish pain and hope:
        remembering  Dr. Korczak shepherding,
        and singing with his beloved 200 orphans,
        dancing to their outing of no return;
        crying for the ninety-three *Beth Jacob Yeshivah* schoolgirls,
        who, like the defenders of Masada,
        collectively sacrificed their innocent lives,
        in sanctification of the Holy Name,
        rather than succumbing
        to the satanic inhumanity of their Nazi captors;
        standing in awe of Ringelblum's depth of compassion;
        saluting Anielewicz and his Warsaw Ghetto freedom fighters;
            paying homage to Rapoport and his monuments of martyrdom.

You're the present-day victory of the Jewish flame,
        imbued by the liberated vision of peace
        of your humble founders:
        Herzl, Nordau, Ahad Haam, Weizmann,
            Jabotinsky, Ben-Gurion, Golda, and Begin.

O Israel, You're the poetry of the universe
        ushering the revival of spirit
        into our own awareness of time and space,
            denoting the motive, motion, meaning, and intent,
        dwelling within the *Shabbat* holiness of Your heritage
            for our everyday application.

Time and again,
        Your prophetic rebirth matters to us,
        throughout the earthly span of our lives,
        as much as the extent, sum, and substance
            of the hallowed eternity, as a whole.

O Israel
> Your sublime flame
>> keeps
>> enlightening
>> all of humanity
>> with
>> the Book
>> penned
> on Your knees.

It projects
>> the messianic visions
>> to be kept alive
>> in the heart
> of the universe.

It proclaims
>> that none
>> shall make
>> the nations
>> on our planet
>> indifferent again
>> to the suffering
>> of the innocent,
>> to the destruction
>> of human life,
>> to the disintegration
>> of freedoms
> and to the debasement of self-respect.

For there is
>> a 4,000-years-of-civilization-untouchable
>> light of universal truth
>> in the collective lights
>> of Your offspring
>> enduring the test of time
>> face-to-face
> with the cycles of nature.

EIGHTEEN GATES BY ISSACHAR MIRON / GATE THIRTEEN: YOM HA-ATZMA'UT / SIX THOUSAND SOULS OF GOLD

Soaring
at the highest altitudes
of courage,
and circling
with the moon
around the earth,
they—the six thousand souls
of Israel's Independence War defenders—
shield with an umbrella of love
the Land for whose revival
they tendered their lives in bloom.

Hiking
on the tunes of time
to their Jerusalem
of eternal promise,
they lean on the synthesis
of the heavenly clouds
that can hug
and the earthly shoulders
that must be put to the wheel.

They dance
and sing with Miriam, David, and Jubal
the songs of *Haganah, Palmah,* and *Beitar*.
They hold hands.
They remember past.
They ponder present.
And they debate the future.

Morning, noon, and night
they watch from their heights
the haunting beauty of Israel.
They sharpen its radiant sanctity,
guarding the heaven and the earth.

They proffer
a bouquet of psalms
for Independence Day.
They shed tears of thanksgiving,
yielding the life-giving rains
to fertilize the arid terrains of *Eretz Yisrael*,
at all heights and valleys of their hearts.
They amen with love your prayers.

Having
opened a new path,
the six thousand souls
of the great dream
inspire us
to hold our ground
with vigilant vision
and to overturn
the fast-moving lava
of Jew-hatred
threatening to engulf
our biblical inheritance
and our existence
among the peoples
of the earth.

Is there anything
more fit for hailing the brave
than sounding
the great *Shofar*
of our freedom
and
bearing in mind
their pain and glory?

Rock and Redeemer of Israel,
bless the State of Israel
and make us worthy
of emulating the spiritual legacy
of the six thousand souls of gold.

Shelter
them under the wings
of Thy tender mercy,
and entrust us
with the privilege of carrying
in our hearts and in our deeds
their pioneering spirit.

May
their valor
and their sacrifice hasten
the arrival of the Messiah,
bringing redemption
for us and for all humanity
and may their memory
be cherished forever.
Amen.

# Ani Ma'amin אני מאמין

**Words: Moses Maimonides**  **Music: Issachar Miron**

## Lag ba-Omer

*Arthur Szyk*

*"The Lord will give strength unto His people;*
*The Lord will bless His people with peace."*

*Psalm 29:11*

# Lag ba-Omer, the Thirty-third Day of the Omer

*Lag ba-Omer, which, on the 18th of Iyyar (coinciding with May), is celebrated by bonfires, weddings, and pilgrimages to Mount Meiron in the Galilee, cancels for a day the semimourning between Passover and Shavu'ot, thought to commemorate Bar Koḥba's rebellion and martyrdom.*

Maimonides welcomed all attempts to build toward a messianic reality, provided that those attempts were realistic. Although he denounced messianic pretenders whose baseless fanaticism merely imperiled the Jewish community, he regarded the Bar Koḥba rebellion as a risk that had been worth taking.

*Rabbi David Hartman*, A Living Covenant
*(The Free Press, A Division of Macmillan, Inc., London, 1985)*

Israeli textbooks portray Bar Koḥba and his rebellion in positive terms. History is embellished. Legendary details entirely unhistorical are added.

*Yehoshafat Harkabi*, The Bar Kokhba Syndrome
*(Rossel Books, Chappaqua, N.Y., 1983)*

The brutal suppression of the Bar Koḥba rebellion by the Emperor Hadrian marks a decisive break in Jewish history. More than 1,800 years would pass before Jews would again be masters of Jerusalem.

*Abba Eban*, Heritage: Civilization and the Jews
*(Summit Books, New York, 1984)*

But if Bar Koḥba would rise from his grave, he would be saluted by the soldiers of modern Judea. . . . But if the Roman commander, whose soldiers had scaled the cliffs to ferret out Bar Koḥba and his men, came to life, what would he find? He would find that the empire he had served had since been washed away in the tide of history and its records existed only in textbooks.

*Yaacov Herzog (1921–1972)*, A People that Dwells Alone
*(Weidenfeld and Nicolson, London, 1975)*

## Gate 14

**"Lag ba-Omer, the Thirty-third Day of the Omer"**

### Gatepost Epigraph

#### *Triumph*

Lag ba-Omer

never succumbed

to nearsightedness,

scrutinizing

under

the microscope

a speck of dust

and perceiving

it

as the wholeness

of the universe.


Thus

it

has triumphed

as the longevity

of a legend

over

irrevocable facts

recorded by History.


From "Longevity of a Legend"

EIGHTEEN GATES BY ISSACHAR MIRON / GATE FOURTEEN: LAG BA-OMER / TRIUMPH

# *Hundred-Generation Saga*

EIGHTEEN GATES BY ISSACHAR MIRON / GATE FOURTEEN: LAG BA-OMER / HUNDRED-GENERATION SAGA

Is it moral
to rejoice
on
a day recalling
the most disastrous defeat
of
our open-ended history?

Didn't the ill-starred
Bar Koḥba revolt
leave
indelible scars of destruction,
marking
in so-many-time-after-times,
the tragic end
of Israel's Second Commonwealth,
and
beginning history's
longest Diaspora with its gruesome woe?

Was
the cessation
of
the ravaging plague
or
paying the ever-timely
tribute
to
a sagacious teacher
sufficient reason
to forget on this day
one of our people's greatest tragedies?

So
what's the reason
for celebrating the day
with picnics, campfires,
dancing and singing?

Isn't it, then,
a self-righteous act
of national self-deception,
or an amnesiac loss
of
historic memory?

Bar Koḥba's legacy
is rooted today
in our perception
of Jewish ways of life
and their proven adherence
to the sacred inviolability of liberty.

It resounded with the heartbeat
of the rescuers
at Entebbe.
It was engraved
by the penmanship
of the heroes of Israel
who sacrificed
their lives
during the Independence War,
during the Six-Day War,
during the Yom Kippur War,
and during
our never-ending quests
for religious,
cultural, social, and political freedoms.

This inheritance
was reflected
in the eyes of the defenders
in the sewers
of the burning Warsaw ghetto
who, in their final hour,
at the bottomless depths
of dirt and death,
raised their voices
in a sunny,
sweet-toned,
yet hard-bitten song,
*"Oif tzeloḥes ale sonim Am Israel Ḥai,"*
joining
with Rabbi Akiva
and his disciples,
the polyphonous choirs of Seraphim,
and bridging the hundred-generation saga
of Jewish martyrdom.

# *Longevity of a Legend*

Lag ba-Omer's
endless vistas
have vindicated
its legacy
of
farsightedness—
an unaided eye
seeing
through
its wide
crystalline lens
the splendors
of
the distant horizon.

Lag ba-Omer
never
succumbed
to nearsightedness,
scrutinizing
under
the microscope
a speck
of dust
and perceiving
it
as the wholeness
of
the universe.

Thus
it
has triumphed
as
the longevity
of
a legend
over
irrevocable facts
recorded
by History.

# *Midrashic Manifesto*

Our heritage,
alternating
light and darkness,
has,
under
the grace
of Providence,
its own sphere of logic,
impervious
to the verdicts of history:
the 33rd day
of *Sefirat ha-Omer*,
which, despite
its legendary appearance,
seems
not to be
a commemoration
of an event.

It is rather
a midrashic
manifesto
of lucid resolve
in an unequal battle
never to be
deterred
by martyrdom
when
defending
the Covenant
of our sacred heritage
and the promise
of the messianic dream.

It is our
subconscious quest
for
the redemption
of Zion
and
the restoration
of our inheritance
in *Eretz Yisrael*.

It has been
our prayer of prayers
for
the rebirth of Israel
as the refuge
and home
for
the remnant
of remnants of our people.

# D'ror Yikra    דרור יקרא
### *Words: Donnah Ben Lavrat Halevi*       *Music: Issachar Miron*

**Energico, moderately with enthusiasm ( ♩ =96)**

D'ror Yik - ra le - ven im bat ve - yin - tzor - ḥem ke - mo va - vat ne -

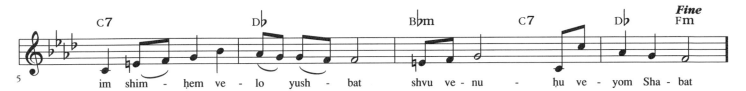

im shim - ḥem ve - lo yush - bat shvu ve - nu - ḥu ve - yom Sha - bat

D'ror Yik - ra le - ven im bat ve - yin - tzor - ḥem ke - mo va - vat ne -

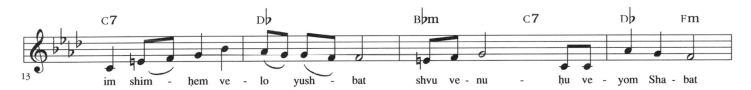

im shim - ḥem ve - lo yush - bat shvu ve - nu - ḥu ve - yom Sha - bat

D'ror Yik - ra_____ D'ror Yik - ra le - ven_____ im_____ bat ve -

yin - tzor - ḥem ke - mo va - vat ke - mo_____ va - vat ne -

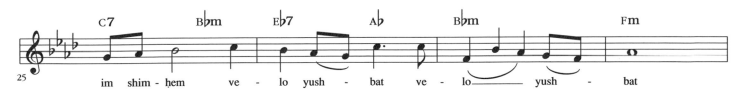

im shim - ḥem ve - lo yush - bat ve - lo_____ yush - bat

shvu ve - nu - ḥu ve - yom Sha - bat ve - yom Sha - bat

***D. C. al Fine***

*Arthur Szyk*

# His Inheritance—Samuel Anointing Saul

*"Is it not that the Lord hath anointed thee*
*to be prince over His inheritance?"*

*1 Samuel 10:1*

# Gate 15
# Yom Yerushalayim, the Day of Jerusalem

*Yom Yerushalayim—the day commemorating the liberation of the Old City of Jerusalem in the Six-Day War, celebrates the reunification of Jerusalem, Israel's capital, on the 28th of Iyyar, 5727 (June 7, 1967). On June 27, 1967, the Knesset enacted the Protection of Holy Places Law ensuring the freedom of access to Jerusalem's Holy Sites to members of all faiths and nations.*

There is a Jerusalem above, corresponding to the Jerusalem below; for sheer love of the earthly Jerusalem, God made himself one above.

*Midrash Tanḥumah (beginning of section Pekudey)*

The idea of the celestial Jerusalem as it was conceived by Jewish thinkers, and even by mystic fancy, never lost its touch with down-to-earth reality.

*Shemaryahu Talmon, The Meaning of Jerusalem, by R. J. Zwi Werblowsky (Israel University Study Group, Jerusalem, 1977)*

Jewish Jerusalem is an organic and inseparable part of the State of Israel, as it is an inseparable part of the history of Israel, the faith of Israel and the soul of our people.

*David Ben-Gurion (1886–1973)*

I was born in Buczacz, but only in a dream; in reality I was born in Jerusalem and exiled by Titus.

*Shmuel Yosef Agnon (1888–1970)*
*(The Nobel prize for Literature, Acceptance Speech, Stockholm, 1966)*

It's good, very good, that the universe should know that our Jerusalem belongs to all.

*Hayim Hefer (1925– ), Yerushalayim Shel Kulam*
*(Edanim, Yedioth Achronoth Edition, Jerusalem, 1978)*

Real, but miraculous to a degree of unreality. One can live in Jerusalem and, at the same time, yearn for it with a burning heart.

*Yehuda Haezrahi, Jerusalem (Spotlight Publications Ltd., Steimatzky's Agency Ltd., Jerusalem, 1972)*

# EIGHTEEN GATES OF JEWISH HOLIDAYS AND FESTIVALS

## Gate 15

**"Yom Yerushalayim, the Day of Jerusalem"**

### Gatepost Epigraph

#### O Undivided, Beautiful City

We pray
that wherever we die
the unfinished score
of our life ascend unto You,
O Undivided, Beautiful City,
joining Your hope trimillennial.

And, we pray that . . .
the vision of our life
be redeemed in Your midst,
revering Your éclat of prophecies,
dipping into Your epic,
singing out unto You
our untapped ecstasies of love.

And, contrariwise,
You are our own *raison d'être*,
and our loftiest reason for living.
You are indeed our beloved home,
O fair crested Joy of all Earth.
*Le'Ḥayim!*

**From "Earthly Custodian"**

# *Higher Than Dreams*

Under the blushing
honey-thick
golden glimmer
of the sunshine-eyed dawn,
some people may go to the City
to look for the untraceable stone
on which Isaiah
might have contemplated
his prophecy of peace.

Mystics and literati
may come here to meditate guiltily
on the psychological complexity
in the vilified and glorified
labyrinths of trial and triumph
leading to the Jewish vivid present tense.

The young and dapper bon vivants
may loll in your Independence Park,
tailgate clouds,
reach out higher than dreams,
picnic in Your greenbelt forests,
visit the archeological sites,
browse through museums and markets,
or flock into Your small cafés
to satiate their craving
for a cup of coffee
or a chat with friends.

Cognoscenti
may juxtapose
the metaphysical ebullience
against the archeological embrace
and be repuzzled
by the endless wars,
interwoven by history
with Jerusalem's never-failing
quest for peace,
and with the millennial mystery
of Her seventy names,
repeating silently
with the evening breezes the Oath:
"If I forget you, O Jerusalem,
let my right hand wither."

# *Earthly Custodian*

Heading for the hills,
enraptured by haunting reveries,
you are embraced
by sonic sophistication
from the Psalmist's harp,
reverberating eternally,
impassioned subtleties
and sweet sensations,
rippling wave-like,
graceful scriptural splendors.

Consoling your sorrow,
you'll extol Jerusalem's glory,
rejoicing again
in the resplendence
of Her unification
under Jewish sovereignty.

Hers the innate gentleness
of the most private
dreams dreamt
by you and every living thing.

She's the City of Truth,
the earthly custodian
of God's holiness,
guarding nine-tenths
of the world's beauty.

We pray
that wherever we die
the unfinished score
of our life ascend unto You,
O Undivided, Beautiful City,
joining Your hope trimillennial.

And, we pray that . . .
the vision of our life
be redeemed in Your midst,
revering Your éclat of prophecies,
dipping into Your epic,
singing out unto You
our untapped ecstasies of love.

And, contrariwise,
You are our own *raison d'être*,
and our loftiest reason for living.
You are indeed our beloved home,
O fair crested Joy of all Earth.
*Le'Ḥayim!*

# *Holiest of All Shrines*

While
the penitent rest-seeking old
meditate
waiting
to die
in Your prophetic midst,
the soul-searching young
open
new windows
to ancient promises,
probing
their landscaped avenues
of self-doubt
at the
one-hundred-ninety-five-foot-long,
most-sky-ceilinged-and-holiest
of all shrines:
Your Wall
sculptured
by winds
of tears and blood
and housing
in its mystical
heart
the Ark
of the Covenant.

Still,
others
of all ages
motivated
by devotion
deeper
than reason—
leaving
unceremoniously
behind them
their previous lives—
return
to Your fold
resounding
with faith.

They
re-create
personal past
casting
their future
in rhythm
with the heartbeat
of their innermost
yearning,
reinventing
for themselves
an invigorated present.

We're
dazzled
by Your
biblical rapport
with the 20th century,
with
Your unflinching
counterpoint
of privacy
and public domain,
grandiosity
and smallness
in Your
invulnerability
and fallibility.

You're
the soul
of our chiefest joy
and
the heavenly modem
built
with a blessing
into
our earthly body,
O Navel
of the Universe,
for
*"God is in the midst*
*of Her,*
*She shall not be*
*tumbled down.*
*God shall help*
*Her,*
*at the approach*
*of morning."*

# *Praying Silently for You*

We're awed
by Your discreet eavesdropping
on the history's fame and infamy,
surviving in Your unique equation
of youthfulness and maturity,
messianic morality
and all-tolerating universality.

As in the days of old,
like a loving mother
with warmth and pettiness,
You're snooping
on the seismic waves
of complexity and simplicity,
sensualized by millennial gossip,
lip-syncing human failings
with divine prophecy
endowed with eternal life.

You're charting routes
through an enticing maze
of brilliance and color
to the unimaginable open-minded
joie de vivre
of Your defiantly controversial
seven earthly gates.

Your willpower,
founded on faith,
is cobbled with dreams,
forged through suffering,
gloried in
our children's grandeur.

Every rock on Zion's Hill
can join a round with a psalm
and with the world
and everything in it,
orchestrating passionate
praises unto the Lord,
shedding an antiphonal tear
and praying silently
for You, O Beautiful City.

# Ha-Yafah sheba-T'filot ה= היפה שבתפילות

**Words: Dan Almagor**  **Music: Issachar Miron**

**Espressivo, with tenderness and dignity**

Sham mul ha-ko-tel bein ha-ho-mot Sham a-hi be-ya-had na-a-mod Nil-

hatz yad el yad li-bei-nu yir-ad ve-no-mar she-he-he-ya-nu ve-kiy-ma-nu

she-le-han hi-ga-nu She-za-hi-nu la-a-lot kvar ba-sha-nah ha-zot li-ru-sha-

la-yim A-hi she - li a-hi ha-tov she-li ma-du-a nam-tin la-sha-

nah——ha-ba-ah U-le-mah od ne-ha-keh Bo na-a-leh mi-yad li-ru-sha-la-yim

Ken a-hi le-hit-ra-ot od ba-sha-nah ha-zot bi-ru-sha-la-yim

Ha-ya-fah she-ba-tfi-lot hi la-sha-nah ha-zot bi-ru-sha-

la-yim la-sha-nah ha-zot bi-ru-sha-la-yim

181

*Arthur Szyk*

*Defense of Tel Ḥai: "If I am not for myself, who is for me?"*

**This saying of Hillel (c. 70 B.C.E.–10 C.E.) epitomized the contribution
of Josef Trumpeldor, the defender of Tel Ḥai (1920) in the Upper Galilee,
to the pioneering spirit of Eretz Yisrael and the inevitability of Jewish self-defense.**

# Gate 16
## Solidarity Day

*Solidarity Day, in May, was inspired by the National Conference on Soviet Jewry and the Greater New York Coalition for Soviet Jewry in an informal but quite effective cooperation with some 300 local Jewish federations and their constituents. In a broader sense this concept of Solidarity Day is now evolving into a day of universal solidarity rather than a specific event, embracing former Soviet, Ethiopian, Syrian, Persian, and Balkan Jews, and oppressed Jews everywhere. The inclusion here of Solidarity Day as a "holiday" celebrates Jewish responsibility for one another, generation after generation, white and black, living in 100 countries around the globe, speaking 70 languages and all yearning to live Jewishly as free people.*

The refuseniks were outcasts from Soviet society, but they were denied the opportunity to be a part of that other society, Israel, which would not only welcome them, but which, under its Law of Return, made legal provision for every Jew in the world who wished to live there to have the automatic right of entry and citizenship.

*Martin Gilbert*, Hero of Our Time
*(Elisabeth Sifton Books—Viking, New York, 1986)*

What's at stake is not only the freedom and the hope of the refuseniks and other dissidents. Our honor is also at stake.

*Elie Wiesel, "What Sharansky Means to the World: Others Need Help" (New York Times, 1986)*

We all wish we could have been able to save Jews from the Nazi Holocaust. Now we can save hundreds of thousands, if not millions, of Jews in the Soviet Union from a final destruction, from an end as a people.

*Anatoly Sharansky*, Miracles & Imperatives. A Guide To Jewish Living 5748 *(New York Times, 1987)*

I knew that the Soviet Union had not succeeded in breaking their spirit, that Russia, with all its power, had failed. The Jews had remained Jews.

*Golda Meir (1898–1978)*

EIGHTEEN GATES OF JEWISH HOLIDAYS AND FESTIVALS

## Gate 16

"Solidarity  Day"

# Gatepost Epigraph

## Notice

Thus,
we post on the walls
of the universe,
on the ceilings
of the sky,
and on the frontiers
of the mind
an eye- and ear-catching
notice of Jewish solidarity,
for all to see and hear:

Whenever
our brothers and sisters—
black and white—suffer,
we'll never fail them.

We'll open to them
our homes
and our hearts
in everything
we have or do,
everywhere
we dwell or go.

From "Black and White"

# *Beware of Truth*

Ever since and long before
    the unthinkable has become speakable,
    I've been the Refuseniks'
    freedom-of-faith supply knapsack,
    fairly filled with the resourcefulness of *Eretz Yisrael*.

I've heralded the dawning
    of direct flights from Moscow to Tel Aviv,
    the unfurling of the blue-and-white flag
    over Israel's embassies in the former Soviet Union.
    I've harbingered the rightful rescission
    of the viper-tongued declaration
    equating Zionism with racism.

Though I'm older than Russia,
    some 70 times the age of the State of Israel,
    well over two millennia,
    more "promised-land" than the American dream,
    pluralistically, mine is still a long way to go.

And though
    commonly seen as a patchwork
    of conflicting historic impulses,
    reciting the eternal *Kaddish*
    for the murdered Jewish poets
    in the KGB's Lubyanka prison,
    I am a credible blueprint of the evolving,
    contemporary color-blind exoduses of all colors;
    glowing like the summer sunrise,
    lighting the paths of the pained and perplexed
    setting their sails in the very eye of multinational storms.

Hence,
    I have prayed for and embraced
    the geopolitical earthquakes,
    carrying the unimaginable beacons of salvation
    from the passivity of repression of spirit
    to the maturity of will in affirmative action.

Is it a dream come true?
    No illusions, we're again at the beginning.
    Yet, in spite of all these years of torment,
    it's for my brothers and sisters
    an open-armed wake-up call of reborn hope.

Metaphysically, I am singing
    freedom sweeter than violins,
    and grammatically, I'm mounting my warning
    to all, imposed by force or freely elected Pharaohs:
    Beware of faith forging forth
    through the earth's subconscious self
    within the totality of time.
    Beware of truth growing out of Zion
    and embracing every living thing.
    Hallelujah!

# Doesn't It Worry You?

If I am the deep-seated resistance
to reigns of terror,
and to the never-to-be-forgotten
state-orchestrated campaigns of vilification,
then mine is the duty to safeguard
our inherent will to live Jewish lives.
Everywhere!

Thus I am
and always will be
the guarantor
of human rights' vigilance
throughout the year.

Though I've welcomed the winds of change,
I'm now deeply troubled
that right from the start
the transformation benefited just the few,
discriminated against the many.

And so far, even worse.
I'm pained that the *glasnost*-minded
liberation has liberated
the untidy *naglost* and anti-Semitism,
and shamelessly will not lift a finger,
nor even utter a peep to stop that hardheaded,
ugly upsurge of racial violence and ethnic purification,
dwarfing its own vision of democracy
into a crumbling-crippling-cruel-civil-rights reality.

All in all, am I hypersensitive?
Doesn't it worry you?
Come on.
What would you expect?
It seems plain.  Surely it worries me.

At this point, getting to the bone—
though my torn flesh is still bleeding—
I shall never be frightened off.
I shall never allow them
to scapegoat you or me again
to save a collapsed empire
in its multiple
independent reincarnations of evilness.

Moreover, not now.
Not now when it's disguised as anti-Israelism.
Not now when hiding under any other dress.
Not now physically.  Not now morally.
Not economically.  Not politically.
Not religioculturally.
Not ever!

# *Self-Deceptive Is Self-Extinctive*

Transmuting
    the contemptuously bigoted ersatz
    of "Jewish-conspiracy" ploys
    into the potent fuel
    of courageous vision for today,
    we've helped
    to roll up the Iron Curtain—
    even before it disintegrated—
    to ensure for our people
    held hostage,
    the right to breathe there in liberty,
    or to leave unintimidated,
        if they want.

For
    if we are
    as youthfully evocative
    as foretold by the Bible,
    we are still the 4,000-year-old
    quest of Jewish togetherness—
        in soul, in mind, and in body.

We are
    the earthly guardian angels
    of the oppressed Jews everywhere,
    whether persecuted by Jew-baiters,
    or used as scapegoats by corruption,
    bearing the brunt of the blame
    in the wilderness of turmoil,
        for sinister swindles committed by others.

And frankly,
    we are the generational resolve
    of the Maccabees,
    who taught us that silence—
    far more than being self-deceptive—
    is self-extinctive.

*"Blessed are You, our Lord,*
*King of the universe,*
*Who has kept us alive,*
*sustained us and brought us to this season."*
    Amen.

# *Troika*

Now, again on the ascent,
    our six-pointed Star of David
        overflowing with belief,
        is casting a golden dawn
        on the prisoners of Zion,
        freed from their *Red* bondage,
        yet still trapped "inside an enigma,"
    amid the gulags of darkness.

David's shield
    awakens a modern-day miracle,
        for the oppressed by the old bigotry
        unmasking now
        the many disguises of a tumbled empire,
        de-Sovietized,
        de-Iron-Curtain-ized—
    yet, still arrogantly desensitized.

Our Star's spirit beams a beacon for our kin
    still despised, still dejected
        by the unreconstructed-by-*perestroika* prejudice
        leaping from one fickle horse to another,
        riding with savage recklessness
        while standing astride
        the four moving-far-apart horses:
            the ethnic infighting,
            the old authoritarianism,
            the combustible nationalism
            and the limping democratization
            (still more fragile than an eggshell),
        dragging now at a sclerotic trot
        behind the *Pamyat*'s wildly galloping *troika*
    of chaos, cruelty, and anti-Semitism.

Then, what has changed?
    With regard to facts, there's at least one difference.
        There's another *troika*
        of our faith, courage, and anger
        unhorsing the narrow-minded ugliness:
            *Firstly*, it's the *strength of insight*
                (we're on guard looking the treachery right in the eye).
            *Secondly*, it's the *inevitability of watchfulness*
                (the world is honing its newborn vigilance).
            *Thirdly*, it's a *warning* enjoining us to bear it in mind
                (and in history that has uttered its verdict).

Isn't it a divine promise?
        So, bring the flame and the roof
            for members of your family—
            wherever homeless or whenever jobless—
            who need today your outstretched hand
            as much as they needed yesterday
        your clenched fist.

Then, move
    heaven and earth,
        lucidly lip-syncing with the Lord
        the hallowed and the healing *"Shema Yisrael."*

# *Black and White*

They and we have surfaced
the too-long-hidden torrents
of the Jewish superconductivity,
matching the pixels of the unity of our being
with the pixels of love on the heavenly screens,
baffling the most astute demographers.

Our Song of Songs of Solomon—
ringing proud in Hebrew, Aramaic, Ge'ez, or Amharic
(millennia before it became fashionably
enlightened to say "black is beautiful") —
is the bias-free proof they weren't forgotten.

Then, for the voiceless—
the Black House of Israel—
an ancient jewel now fully restored
to the crown of Jerusalem,
ours has been the voice of liberty.

By airlifting them to the Promised Land
via a modern-day Exodus above the Red Sea,
we remain the fountainhead of relief for them,
the forlorn still called by their neighbors
after 2,500 years "falashas"—strangers!—
now being woven into Zion's tapestry
of our national being.

Despite being weighed down by pain,
despite the angry tornadoes,
the earthquakes of bigotry still pounding us daily,
our unshackled hope strengthens itself to grow taller
and readier for the cosmic battles
in the global wilds of life,
and within the ultraprivate niches of our hearts.

In earnest, despite all these tremors,
abstract foreshocks and concrete aftershocks,
shuddering every season the earths of our being,
we dare not . . . not set the vow of our loving oneness
as our topmost commitment,
nor not broadcast to the streetwise world
a warning incarnating on each stratum
in all colors of the spectrum the biblical injunction
not to turn from the true course
of justice and brotherly love.

Thus, we post on the walls of the universe,
on the ceilings of the sky,
and on the frontiers of the mind
an eye- and ear-catching notice of Jewish solidarity,
for all to see and hear:

Whenever our brothers and sisters—
black and white—suffer, we'll never fail them.

We'll open to them our homes and our hearts
in everything we have or do,
everywhere we dwell or go.

# *Trust Is Not Enough*

Who would have thought
    that,
    though they—
    our brothers and sisters—
    have just begun
    their 20th-century messianic
    exodus to freedom,
    they would be still threatened,
    isolated,
    hideously inhibited,
    and fearing for their lives
    within
    the foaming
    and bucking borders
        of their swiftly-name-and-face-lifting country?

And who would
    have imagined
    (even in a bad dream)
    that they would be again enduring
    the plural pains of oppression
    inflicted
    by the new reincarnations
    of the dismantled Union—
    now disrobed
    by the half-hearted reforms,
    bankrupted by
    illusionary perspectives,
    stirring in distorted ecstasy,
    rousing a new chaos,
    exciting old fears,
    and denuding
    the heightened old Jew hatred
    well and alive in the new Commonwealth—
        beneath the shamed-to-the-red-blush horizon?

Relating
    to the cause of the disease,
    rather than to its symptoms,
    for its own protection and peace of mind,
    what the threatened world owes it to itself,
    is to remember—with or without conscious awareness—
    that in dealing with tyrants
    on each terrain and/or under any disguise,
        trust is not enough.

# Agudah Aḥat אגודה אחת

*Words: Dan Almagor*  *Music: Issachar Miron*

## Shavu'ot

*"Be strong, be strong, and we will all be stronger."*
*A congratulatory exlamation by the congregation*
*to the Torah reader, made on the completion*
*of each book of the Pentateuch.*

# Gate 17
## Shavu'ot, the Feast of Weeks

*Shavu'ot, the festival commemorating the giving of the Torah on Mount Sinai is also celebrated as Hag ha-Katzir—the Harvest Festival, and Yom ha-Bikkurim—the Day of the First Fruits. Shavu'ot is observed on the 6th of Sivan (May–June).*

Judaism is the national creative power, which has expressed itself in a primarily religious culture.

*Ahad Haam (Asher Ginsberg) (1856–1927)*

When God gave the Torah, no bird sang or flew, no ox bellowed, the angels did not fly and the Seraphim ceased from saying, "Holy, Holy, Holy." The sea was calm, no creature spoke; the world was silent and still and the Divine Voice said: "I am the Lord your God."

*Midrash (Exodus Rabbah, Yitro 29:9)*

And thou shalt keep the feast of weeks unto the Lord thy God after the measure of the free will-offering of thy hand, which thou shalt give, according as the Lord thy God blesseth thee.

*Deuteronomy 16:10*

Why did God choose to appear to Moses in a bush? To show his modesty: The bush is the smallest and most insignificant of trees. And also to underline the symbolical aspects of the event: The bush is Israel. And just as the bird cannot penetrate the bush without getting caught on its thorns, the enemies of Israel will not be able to harm it without being wounded.

*Elie Wiesel*, Messengers of God—Biblical Portraits and Legends
*(Random House, New York, 1976)*

## Gate 17

### "Shavu'ot, the Feast of Weeks"

# Gatepost Epigraph

### Streets of Our Mind

Reflecting

upon the Holy Writ,

from that Solemn Holiday on,

may Thou

*"Who has kept us alive,*

*sustained us,*

*and brought us to this season"*

bless us

with wisdom and freedom

to apply and revivify

the Time of the Giving

of our Torah—

with its built-in upgradability—

in our communities,

dwellings, backyards,

kindergartens, universities,

and on the entwined

streets of our mind.

Hallelujah!

From "Burning Bush"

And who knows?
Some thirty-three centuries ago
on Mount Sinai's crest,
just before the desert caucus
a Ministering Angels Summit Sub-Committee
might have pointed out to the Lord
that attention-getters more durable
than the Two Tablets
ought to be gotten
so that His commandments
should never be forgotten.

After some meditative throat-clearing,
on the spur of the Holy Moment
the Lord might have said to the angels:
Is it Me you're asking?
You yourselves—since I gave you wings—
have preached that what counts
is the message, not the modem,
not a discrete detail
but the soul of the whole
and yet . . . with My children you never know,
so to make Moses' task easier
and My Package of Dos and Don'ts
palatable to all . . .
go and plant there on the top
the Burning Bush judiciously
glaring and declaring My Law—
in Sound, in Word and Image—
to ratify and amplify
the covenantal treaty
that binds Me
and the Seed of Abraham, for eternity.

Then, on second thought,
the Lord—with a mischievous smile—
might even have said to the angels:
Go and tell Moses to shatter
the two tablets of stone in front of the conclave
and scatter their debris for all to see
the essence and endurance
of the Infinite Decree
over its perishable vessel
to exhibit all there's to it:
the supremeness of spirit
and its audiovisual independence
from the earthly substance.

Amen to that.  And so it was.
Henceforth, hail to Thee,
the Hallowed Convocation
on the top
of the Mount
(dramatized
by thunder,
lightning from afar,
and
the sounds of *Shofar*)
was,
is, and shall always be
the multimedia illumination
of
the Divine Revelation.

As it may seem,
our pledge to serve Him
granted the world the privilege
of learning the Lord's Law,
to see and hold in esteem
the eye-opening beam
of the Ten Commandments,
to hear—every day in any way—
their prayerable playback,
while recording and  broadcasting
in seventy languages
their portrayable proclamation
on airwaves, cellular services,
and interactive satellites
for universal application.

Reflecting
upon the Holy Writ,
from that Solemn Holiday on,
may Thou
*"Who has kept us alive,
sustained us,
and brought us to this season"*
bless us
with wisdom and freedom
to apply and revivify
the Time of the Giving
of our Torah—
with its built-in upgradability—
in our communities,
dwellings, backyards,
kindergartens, universities,
and on the entwined
streets of our mind.
Hallelujah!

# *Heart-to-Heart Talk*

Rejoicing
> "In the courts
> of the Lord's house,
> in the midst
> of thee, O Jerusalem,"
> we bring
> with our summertime processions
> of the Feast of the Harvest,
> this thanksgiving unto Thee
> in the everlasting
> spheres of faith
> and well within the mortal range
> > of our sights.

Inherently we celebrate
> Shav'uot
> as the Birthday of Judaism.
> It is the core
> of our greatest blessing,
> affirming that Thou—
> the Creator of the Law—
> > art our Father.

Awaiting
> the coming of Messiah
> and saying the daily
> portion of the Psalms,
> as Your children
> we have the right
> to rededicate ourselves
> to learn Your Torah,
> to improve our ways,
> to plead any grievance,
> to express our frustration,
> to file a complaint,
> to have with Thee
> a heart-to-heart talk,
> to hug and kiss Thee,
> and to cry on
> > Thy Shoulder.

So, reciting songs of praise
> and eating fruit,
> dairy products and honey,
> we can raise today—
> from our own free will—
> this ever-loving supplication
> to Thee:
> O Forgiving Creator and Lawgiver.

# *Landscaping Mankind's Horizons*

It might
be a fateful event,
but it's fortuitous,
and it epitomizes
curious contrasts,
reversals and triumphs,
that the hallowed season
of Giving the Law
coincides
with the ever-living bloom
of the harvest.

Rain or shine,
Torah
must then be
tilled and tended
every day,
with dedication and diligence,
like the work
of the field.

Only
by our sowing
and growing
the flower beds of goodness,
the four biblical chapters
can burst
with multicolored blossom
within
the eighty-five verses
of the Book of Ruth.

Landscaping
mankind's horizons,
Shavu'ot binds land,
sea and sky in belief,
harvesting
trust in ourselves
and all the others.

It mirrors the greatest
miracle of our being,
the most splendid
of all blessings,
the effluent fountainhead
of the never-failing stream of justice,
the reenactment
of the six days of creation
and the sanctification of *Shabbat*
every growing-up moment
of our lives.

# *His Gardeners*

For the sake
    of teaching
    little children
    the light of truth,
    the Lord
    has given the world
    the efflorescent
        discipline
        of endurance
        for renewal.

For the purpose
    of planting
    in all the hearts that care
    the art of pastoral
    rededication,
    the Lord painted
    the Rose of His universes—
        our beloved
        Mother Earth—
        with all shades
        of rainbowy purity,
        pollinated it
        by peace,
        and entrusted it
            to all of us
            by appointing us
            His rosarian gardeners.

Then the Lord
    has instructed us
    to water with affection
    this rosily prickly stemmed,
    protectively ozone-leaved,
        sowed
        by suffering,
        flowered-by-faith planet—
        and to tend it,
        to prune it,
        and to make it
        bloom,
        preserving
        its profusion
        of divine ecology
            (a command never to be rescinded
            on account of human necessities).

By design, in contemplation
of the budding testimony
of our husbandry civilization,
the Lord commanded
the arable parables
in the nurseries of spirit
to tell us their story
and to teach us by example
how to grow on our own—
the most collective seeds of human experience.

With no optical simulation,
revealing the patterns of life more perceptively than
Computerized Axial Tomography would ever do,
clearer than Digital Audio Tape
would ever sound,
the Lord ordered us to travel by far faster
than the invisible electretic waves
would ever surge,
toward His Personal Insight
dwelling in the Torah
and chanting His cantillations
in our tillable sunshines of salvation.

I believe that faith can illuminate
the past for the memory of it,
rouse the present to action for the survival of it,
lengthen the horizons
of the future for the promise of it,
grow a tree for the shade of it,
nurture our trust in others
for the joy of it.

And, I believe that together we can
nourish freedom for the taste of it,
nurse friendship
for the touch of it,
and embrace the universe
for the peace of it.

Never letting spiritual bygones be bygones,
we can conjure hopeful tomorrows
out of yesterday's pain,
affirming faith with faith.

Where there's a dream
there is a song to awaken the voice,
a melody to restore the will,
and a flame to illuminate the way.

So I believe that jointly
we can open the Lord's life-giving gates,
turning the divine streams of light and love
onto the salvation-thirsty deserts of our being.

May this be our goal now and ever after.

# Shir ha-Be'er שיר הבאר

*Words: Yehiel Haggiz*       *Music: Issachar Miron*

**Battle of Jerusalem**

*Arthur Szyk*

"*Pray for the peace of Jerusalem;*
*May they prosper that love Thee.*"

*Psalm 122:6*

*Tishah be-Av commemorates the destruction of the First (422 B.C.E.) and Second (70 C.E.) Holy Temples of Jerusalem, which were both razed on the Ninth of Av, five centuries apart.*

The martyrs of all ages are sitting at the gates of heaven, having refused to enter the world to come, lest they forget Israel's pledge given in and for this world.

*Abraham Joshua Heschel*, Israel, Jerusalem—Charismatic City
*(Farrar, Straus & Giroux, New York, 1967)*

In hours of clarity, man has come to understand that what he likes to call the progress of the human race does not proceed along the highroad at all. Rather we must set out ever again making our way precariously along a narrow ridge between abysses.

*Martin Buber (1878–1965)*

What are they doing here? And why are they crying? I do not know. They themselves neither know nor say. They see nothing—except the Wall before them. But it is theirs, for it is they who bore it on their shoulders year after year and generation after generation. And their tears—are the Wall's.

*Elie Wiesel (1928–), As If in a Dream*
*(first published in* Hadassah *magazine)*

The Wall is broken and incomplete. It has been deliberately kept that way. Every Jew should be free to finish it the way he wants, with his own dreams and hope.

*Rabbi David Hartman* (New York Times)

How just it happens that paratroopers cry? / How just it happens that they caress the Wall with deep feeling? / How just it happens that their tears turn into song? / Maybe it's because these boys of nineteen, / being born at the same age as the State, / carry on top of their backs—two thousand years.

*Hayim Hefer (1925–) (Yedioth Achronoth, Tel Aviv, 1967)*

Gate 18

"Tishah be-Av, the Fast of the Ninth of Av"

# Gatepost Epigraph

### Faith and Freedom

Elucidating

transpersonal universality,

Tishah be-Av

sprang

like

hope eternal

from

the rubble

of destruction,

turning

the day

of deepest sadness

into

the ascending chord sequences

of bred-in-the-bone integrity

of our distinctiveness,

breathing

in the grace

of infinite

faith

and freedom.

From "Reawakening Dormant Dreams"

# *Evocation of Life*

Bewailing with *kinot*,
in somber verse,
the enormity of desolation,
we mourn the destruction
of the First—and the Second—Holy Temples,
that were both burned to the ground—
six hundred fifty-six years apart,
on the Ninth of *Av*—
convulsing
the world with shock waves of pain,
and slashing the skies
with tear-filled tremolos
of unanswered prayers.

Yet, beyond human understanding—
in omnipresent testimony
to the infinity of faith,
the fire that flattened
every house and tree in Jerusalem
was replete with remorse,
realizing
the ruthless monstrosity
of this calamity,
and therefore safeguarded,
amid ruins,
the Western Wall for eternity.

Aching
for the misfortune and martyrdom
of the dearly beloved
who perished
*Al Kiddush Hashem*,
the mighty flames
forced by the enemy to scourge
the Hallowed Walls
made a surreal U-turn,
taking
their own full-bodied revenge
by tumbling the victor's illusion
into the reality of ashes
and letting him drown
in the immutability of Cainitic shame.

Wasn't it a providential act
igniting
the dawn of Jewish mysticism
and strengthening the resolve
to await the arrival
of the Messiah—Prince of Peace?

*"And although he may tarry,
we await him every day."*
May he come in our time
as an evocation of life.

# Reawakening Dormant Dreams

With uninhibited directness
        and dizzying passion,
        the flames that painted
        the skies red—
        an unabashed quest
        for renewal that never ends,
        in modulation of brotherly love—
        kindled one-to-one
        the timeless challenge
        for purity of aspirations,
        restoring
        the transcendent radiance
        of the Holy Temple
        in millions of Jewish hearts,
        reawakening dormant dreams,
        and reinvigorating
        the nevermore-to-be-diminished
            light of independence.

Elucidating
        transpersonal universality,
        Tish'ah  be-Av
        sprang like hope eternal
        from the rubble of destruction,
        turning
        the day of deepest sadness
        into the ascending chord sequences
        of bred-in-the-bone integrity
        of our distinctiveness,
        breathing in the grace
            of infinite faith and freedom.

It  generates
        in every moment of our being
        irrepressible energy imploring:
        beware the gulf that separates
        the emptiness of unfulfilled life
            from the inner rewards of salvation.

Like Psalms, the Day of Fast
        renders a deft warning
        and sagacious advice to humans
        on how to prevent
        such an inhuman tragedy
            from happening again.

# *Self-Holocaust?*

EIGHTEEN GATES BY ISSACHAR MIRON / GATE EIGHTEEN: TISHAH BE-AV / SELF-HOLOCAUST?

Yet,
after our perilous journey
of two millennia,
the moral
of
the Ninth of the month of *Av*
is still youthful,
sheltering
the shatterproof chests
of our history's
surrealistic collages,
its biomorphic
sense of sanity,
safeguarded for posterity
on
the  treasured bookshelves—
in our hearts.

Is
there an element of hope?

No guessing.

Isn't it then incumbent
upon us
as inhabitants of this planet
to recognize the inevitable?

Unless we put
our collective shoulders
to the
divine, yet injury-prone,
participatory wheels
of free
and fair human rights
for all,
the multiple worlds
of our orbiting being
may halt.

Isn't it then clear
that the cosmic,
ever-present danger
of a nuclear-winter Tish'ah  be-Av,
if not averted,
may sweep down
into our living surroundings
the misery and destruction
of the unutterable hell
of self-holocaust?

# Tomorrow Is Too Late

Hard lessons?
    For all?
        For all.

When chanting
    this evening
    the Book of Lamentations wailing,
    wearing
    this afternoon *tefillin*
    and wrapped
    in the *tallit* praying,
    lest we forget:
        for five billion today.

And
    tomorrow?
    Just think
        of the unthinkable:

As in . . .
    a horror movie,
    everything
    on the global computer of life
    is irreversibly overwritten
    and deleted;
    a crippling power lapse
    fatal to every living thing
    upon earth
        idles the Universe!

Yet still,
    it's quite plain.
    Today it may be your
    last opportunity
    to give your personal contribution
        to *Tikkun Olam.*

Today it may be
    your ultimate occasion to
    *"perfect the universe*
        *in the Kingdom of the Lord."*

Today is your final chance
    to help bring
    to all peoples
    the breadth and depth
    of the morningtide
        breathing redemption.

Our mandate to act
    *right now*
    is none too soon.
        Tomorrow is too late!

# Lamah Bat Tzion?  ? למה בת ציון

*Words: Israel Nag'ara     Music: Issachar Miron*

צאת במצרים

**Exodus**

Arthur Szyk

*"Exile resembles night and redemption is likened unto dawn."*
Psalm 122:6

# Looking into the Future:
## Beyond the Gates, Above Gravitation, Across Time and Space

*The Jewish holidays' and festivals' heritage extends beyond the set dates for commemoration and celebration. It is this heritage that inspires us to look beyond the gates, above the gravitation, and to carry its message across time and space.*

Job personified man's eternal quest for justice and truth—he did not choose resignation. Thus he did not suffer in vain; thanks to him, we know that it is given to man to transform divine injustice into human justice and compassion.

*Elie Wiesel*, Messengers of God
*(Random House, New York, 1976)*

We had come forth from slavery to freedom. On the morrow the sun would shine. And Jewish children once more would laugh.

*Menachem Begin (1913–1992)*, The Revolt
*(Nash Publishing, Los Angeles, 1972)*

Israel realizes that her faith is integrated with the faith of all humanity, that her peace on peace among nations. The heritage of her prophets and the vision of the latter days—as expressed by Micah and Isaiah—guide her steps on the international scæne.

*David Ben Gurion*, The Jews and the Land *(A Windfall Book, Doubleday & Company, Inc., Garden City, New York)*

But the prayer is only a vision, and the vision is but a dream. For, still, clamor is heard in the streets, and weeping, as for an only child. And man conquers the space beyond, but fails to master the island within.

*Libretto and Lyrics: Avraham Soltes (1917–1983)*
*Music: Issachar Miron (1920–)*
Golden Gates of Joy Oratorio
*(Warner/Chappell Music Inc., New York, 1967)*

For a small moment have I forsaken thee; but with great compassion will I gather thee. In a little wrath I hid My face from thee for a moment; but with everlasting kindness will I have compassion on thee, saith the Lord thy Redeemer.

*Isaiah 54:7–8*

EIGHTEEN GATES OF JEWISH HOLIDAYS AND FESTIVALS

## EIGHTEEN GATES

**"Beyond the Gates,
Above Gravitation, Across Time and Space"**

### Gatepost Epigraph

**Sweetest Glissando**

May

the voice

of our conscious

supplication

in tune

with

our collective

*Ani Ma'amin*

ascend

as fast

as

the sweetest glissando

unto

Your ear,

O Lord.

From "Harp and Shield"

# *Confluent Courtship*

May
  our
   perplexed thoughts
   entangled
   in
    the interwoven webs
    of
     the seek-dig-and-discover
     Covenant
<u>underscore</u>
    the cadence of faith
    of the proverbial "*a pintele Yid*"—
    (the never-oppressed-tiniest bit of a Jew
    dwelling eternally within me and you)—
   rooted
  in the undiminished
  ecstatic urgency
 of our softest,
silkiest, breath-whispered
fondness and faithfulness to You.

May
   our deeds soar
  to the heights,
 evoking
 the ever-pliant
romantic timbre
of our
  confluent courtship
  with You.

And
  may the mutuality
  of our warm feelings
   for each other
    grow stronger,
     like a bird fluttering up
      the tree trunk of life,
       and spinning out
 the c r e s c e n d o
    vision of a messianic future
    that, like the tongues of flame,
   will burn
    inside the new frontiers of heart
   and never be consumed,
  wakening the guardians
 of the dream,
dawn by dawn.

# *Harp and Shield*

You
who redeem
our parents,
siblings, and all of us
from dissonance to consonance,
may You cause our humble melody
to convey the prayerful chorale
of our poetic gratitude to You
unaltered, unembellished, undivided.

May You cause
the harmony
played on the highest strings
of our souls to ring out
forcefully
with the lowest strings of our hearts,
cleansing our sins away.

And may You
bring sustained joy
to flourish unintimidated
with the flowers
in the day-by-day gardens of our lives,
helping us
to bridge the post-Holocaust
gulfs of pain and hollowness.

May
the voice
of our conscious supplication
in tune with our collective
*Ani Ma'amin*
ascend
as fast as the sweetest glissando
unto Your ear, O Lord.

Blessed are You,
Harp and Shield
of the universe,
for finding for us ways
to keep our heritage alive
within our seventy-odd languages,
ancient antagonisms, modern afflictions,
magnanimity of spirit, pettiness of mind,
never-failing faith:
all covered by a coat of hope
interlaced with many colors.
Welcome home.
Amen!

# D'ma'ot Gil

*Klezmer-Instrumental*

דמעות גיל

*Music: Issachar Miron*

# *From My Angle*

*by*

## *Hayim Hefer*

Some forty years ago Nathan Alterman, the late, much-revered Israeli poet, introduced me to Issachar Miron, then known as Issachar Michrovsky. Issachar had composed, at that time, some of the most brilliant tunes for Tel Aviv's renowned musical theater, *Li-La-Lo*.

He was already world-acclaimed for his international super hit, *Tzena-Tzena-Tzena,* which invaded Europe with the *Jewish Brigade of the British Army* during World War II and became a great war song of the Allied Forces. His song was brought back home at the end of the war by soldiers of the *Brigade* as a badge of their resilient Jewish identification—a victory song that caught on fire across the entire country, that later spinned with millions of records around the world.

I was then still writing the lyrics of underground songs that were sung clandestinely around the *Palmach* campfires, yet Miron seemed to know every word I ever wrote.

Miron's melodies and my lyrics met for the first time at *Li-La-Lo,* in a hall named for Jasha Heifetz. It was an inspiring joint effort. We were both searching for a new spirit, a new-old rhythm for our tradition, a new style befitting the great epoch of challenge and hope between the ashes and dust of the Holocaust, which had just started to settle, and the roses of Israel's independence, which had not bloomed as yet.

I was drawn to Miron's deep roots in the *Klezmer* musical tradition. In turn, I think he was attracted by the *Sabra* inflections of my Hebrew verse.

Many years have passed since then. We have both gone our own ways, occasionally collaborating here and there. As I write this, I have before me Miron's *Eighteen Gates,* the book of modern prayers, greetings, holy-day meditations and poetry he wrote, enhancing it with some of his moving liturgical compositions.

Resounding its affirmation in a mosaic of moods, *Eighteen Gates* sings with zest for life, reverberates with self-rejuvenating progressions of harmonies in words as in music, commutes between the past and the future, dares a timely style for today, carries on an unrelenting search for a new-old rhythm, mingling tears of pain with tears of promise, and leaping with a brisk step forward.

Issachar Miron, you've got it all. ∎

*Arthur Szyk*

# The Question

**"Why is this night
different
from all other nights?"**

*The Passover Haggadah*

# Epilogue

*by*

# *Rabbi Irving "Yitz" Greenberg*

After thirty-five hundred years and countless interpretations, does anyone seriously hope to offer new insights into the Jewish holidays? Yet the holy days are at the core of Judaism. Enter them and you have discovered the inner sanctum of Judaism itself. Grasp them and you hold the heart of the faith in your hand. Issachar Miron, a leading liturgical composer, contributes to this millennial process in words as in music *"the sweetness of a velvety voice of many colors to participate as full-fledged partners in life's four-part harmony with You, O Lord of Hosts, with our brothers and sisters, and with Your Holy Days"* ("Four-Part Harmony").

It is through its holidays that Judaism is the most visible and most easily accessible. To celebrate the holidays is to live as a Jew by reliving the Jewish way. Judaism's memories, its structures of meaning and its values for living have attained their classic expression in the holidays.

By interpreting and reinterpreting the holidays and applying their lessons to daily life, the Jewish people have been guided and inspired to walk continuously along the Jewish way. This *perush* is reflected by Miron in "Picture-Phone Thank-You Call": *"Thus hiking into the high-hidden country sprawling across the eyewitness-telescopic meadows, we place on the wings of our silent meditation this picture-phone thank-You call—face-to-face-eye-to-eye-ear-to-ear— for consecrating and culling the Hebrew language from the world's 3,000 tongues as the holy vernacular of Your Book."*

There are times when Judaism brings painful memories: moral, problematic conflict with others, obligations so great that we feel guilty no matter what we accomplish.

Yet, on balance, Judaism's overwhelming effect has been to fill our lives with a sense of divine presence and human continuity, of bondedness and joy. In "Song of Love" we find ourselves *gazing upward into the riddle of the night embedded in each and every day [and climbing] through rugged terrain, to see from the promontories of the New Moon the distant habitats of the new dawn in the nearness of our hearts."*

Issachar Miron's *Eighteen Gates* is a thought-provoking collection of all types of contemporary "liturgies" for the Jewish holidays. They help us respond to the Jewish memories, to the conflicts and obligations, to the divine presence and human continuity that are so much the possession of *Amha*—the Jewish people.

The detailed living experiences full of love that make everything worthwhile are particularly found in the Jewish holidays. For the holy days are the quintessential Jewish religious expression; the main teachings of Judaism are incorporated in their messages. Regular experience of these days has sustained the Jews along the long march of Jewish history.

As the holidays are, so is this book intended for *Klal Yisrael,* the whole Jewish people. Miron writes in "Way of Life": *"Isn't our responsibility for each other a way of life rather than merely a mode of existence?"* Pressing this point further, in "Heavenly Microchips," he portrays this generation's commitment to Judaism: *"We harmonize with You—an earth-to-heaven holographic song harnessing our spirituality from each angle. On every level, in three dimensions: in thought, in tendency and in tone, we download at lightning speed Your Word-processing software into the computer-driven program of our mind to upgrade and decode the tenets of Your Heavenly Microchips."*

It is through such fertile expressiveness as is found in this resourceful book, through singing a new song to the Lord in each generation, that the joys and the many forms of observance of our Jewish holidays have enabled us to continue living as Jews from generation to generation, and inspired us with the will to be a light to the nations. ∎

*In memory of my mother, Haya Helen Michrowski, who died at the age of thirty-six, in the bloom of her life, when I was seven years old*

# Misaviv la-Olam

מסביב לעולם

*Klezmer-Instrumental*

*Music: Issachar Miron*

### Moderato, heartily with vigor and a Ḥassidic fervor ( ♩ =88 )

*In memory of my father and mentor, Rabbi Shlomo Michrowski, one of the Holocaust's six million souls of gold, who perished in the death camp of Chelmno*

# Niggun Shlomo

ניגון שלמה

*Klezmer-Instrumental*

Music: Issachar Miron

**Ardently, with a yeshivah-klezmer lilt ( ♩ =88 )**

*by*

## *Arthur Szyk*

# *Alphabetical List of Zemirot and Niggunim*

**Agudah Aḥat** אגודה אחת     **191**

> *Words: Dan Almagor; Music: Issachar Miron*
>
> We are fragile when disunited. In unity—we're invincible. This song was a campaign theme of the United Jewish Appeal campaign, 1973–1983.

**Ani Ma'amin** אני מאמין     **163**

> *Words: Moses Maimonides; Music: Issachar Miron*
>
> From the "Thirteen Principles of Faith": "I believe in perfect faith in the coming of Messiah. And though he may be tardy in coming, I still do believe and await his arrival any day." This song was among the winning entries of the Hasidic Festival of Israel.

**Avinu Malkeinu** אבינו מלכינו     **49**

> *From the Ten Days of Penitence Liturgy. Music: Issachar Miron*
>
> "Our Father, our King, we have no king beside You. Our Father, our King, for Your own sake have mercy on us!" (*Ta'anit 25b, Mishnah*).

**B'raḥot Ḥanukkah** ברכות חנוכה     **97**

> *Ḥanukkah Liturgy. Music: Issachar Miron*
>
> "Blessed are You, our God, King of the universe, Who has sanctified us with His commandments, and has commanded us to kindle the Ḥanukkah light."

**D'ma'ot Gil** דמעות גיל     **215**

> *Klezmer-instrumental. Music: Issachar Miron*
>
> If tears mirror feelings, than tears of joy are humanely dearest like the tears of happiness glimmering in the bride's eyes. It's *niggun* for a wedding or any other joyful occasion.

**Shir ha-Be'er**  שיר הבאר                                                                 **201**

*Words: Yehiel Haggiz; Music: Issachar Miron*

"And to ev'ryone we'll tell, "water, water's in the well!" Too
profound it is to sound it, waters' depth, so fresh and pure. All
around, in plains and mountains, there's no well like this for
sure." (From the English translation by Harry Arvey)

**Shir Shabbat**  שיר שבת                                                                    **31**

*Words: Shimshon Halfi; Music: Issachar Miron*

The Sabbath as seen from a farmer's-eye view. The village and the
field are still restfully asleep. The awakening sun is sending its
blessing to earth.

**Sim Shalom**  שים שלום                                                                     **21**

*From the Liturgy. Music: Issachar Miron*

"Our Father, grant peace with welfare and blessing, and grace
with lovingkindness and mercy on us and on all Israel Thy
people." Also well known in its instrumental *Klezmer* version.

**Sisu ve-Simḥu**  שישו ושמחו                                                                **75**

*Hakkafah-Circuits, Simḥat Torah Liturgy.    Music:
Issachar Miron*

"Rejoice and be glad with the celebration of the Torah, and pay
homage to the Torah, for it is better than any commerce, more
precious than finest gold and jewels." This liturgical theme has
become associated not only with Simḥat Torah, but with a great
variety of joyous occasions and festivals in contemporary Israel—celebrating every day as the divine gift of the Torah.

**Va-Anaḥnu**  ואנחנו                                                                        **63**

*From Aleinu. Music: Issachar Miron*

"For we bow in worship before the supreme King of kings, the
Holy one, the blessed one." From the oratorio service, *D'ror
Yikra*, a service for Sabbath Eve and Sabbath Ḥanukkah.

# Glossary

**Al Kiddush ha-Shem:**
> Martyrdom for the sanctification of the Lord's Holy Name. ("Evocation of Life," page 205.)

**Amalek:**
> Refers today to any vicious anti-Semite. Amalek, a tribe in ancient Philistia, on the southeast coast of the Mediterranean, was a deceitful enemy of the Israelites. Deuteronomy 25:17 exhorts, "Remember what Amalek did unto thee by the way ye came forth out of Egypt." On Purim, whenever Haman's name is mentioned, the congregants rattle their *greggers* (noisemakers) as a mode of interpreting the Deuteronomy 25:19 injunction, "Thou shalt blot out the remembrance of Amalek from under heaven." Amalek is believed to have been Haman's ancestor. ("Downplayed Pain," page 112.)

**"Angel-Leviathans of the Sea":**
> A reference alluding to the biblical moral of Jacob wrestling the angel (Genesis 32:25-29). ("Welcome Aboard," page 42.)

**Ani Ma'amin:**
> "I do believe," from Maimonides' "Thirteen Principles of Faith." "I do believe in perfect faith in the coming of Messiah. And though he may be tardy in coming, I still do believe and await his arrival every day." ("Oasis," page 96.)

**Aravah (plural, Aravot):**
> The two ceremonial willow branches for Sukkot, the Festival of Tabernacles.

**Architectonic wonders:**
> "And they built for Pharaoh store-cities, Pithom and Raamses" (Exodus 1:11). ("Tête-à-Tête with Eternity," page 132.)

**"Assessment in Retrospect":**
> In the spirit of ". . . we will do and listen" (Exodus 24:7), implying the primacy of obedience to the Lord's commandments, to be followed by the privilege of study and assessment in retrospect. ("New Beginning," page 44.)

**Bar Kohba:**
> Leader of the heroic revolt against the Romans, 135 B.C.E., that ended in catastrophe and has been regarded by some historians as ill advised, as voiced in our generation by Prof. Yehoshafat Harkabi, an eminent scholar and general (Ret.) in the Israel Defense Force.

**Beitar:**
> A paramilitary youth organization (an acronym for *Yosef Trumpeldor's Hebrew Youth Society*) associated with the Revisionist Movement; many of its members were among the founders of *Irgun Zvai Leumi* and *Lohamei Herut Israel*, liberation movements in prestate Israel.

**Be-te'avon:**

> A Hebrew equivalent to the French *bon appétit*—we wish you a hearty appetite.

**Bimah:**

> The Torah Reader's platform, usually located in the center of the synagogue, from which liturgical proceedings are conducted—mostly the reading of the Torah itself.

**Blessed Are You:**

> A thanksgiving Ḥanukkah Blessing: "Blessed are You, our Lord, King of the universe, Who has kept us alive, and sustained us, and brought us to this season." ("Self-Deceptive Is Self-Extinctive," page 187.)

**Book of Life** (in Hebrew, *Sefer ha-Ḥayim*)**:**

> A heavenly kept record of every human being's conduct throughout the year that contains three ledgers of "Life," of "Death," and of "Suspended for Scrutiny" on the Day of Atonement.

**Chełmno:**

> The first Nazi death camp for mass killing in Poland, in the district of Koło (the vicinity of Kalisz), where 320,000 Jews were murdered during the Holocaust (1941–1945), initially in large grey gas-vans equipped with built-in poison gas chambers, "airtight doors, metal-lined and floored with duck-boards under which were visible the wire-gauze covered ends of tubes connected with an outside apparatus operated by the German Gestapo drivers," according to the eyewitness testimony published in the 1943 *Black Book of Polish Jewry*.

**City of Truth:**

> "Jerusalem shall be called the city of truth" (Zechariah 8:3). ("Earthly Custodian," page 176.)

**Concordat:**

> The July 20, 1933, agreement between the Holy See and Hitler's Third Reich designed to protect the Roman Catholic Church's rights under the Nazi regime.

**David's harp:**

> David, Israel's second king, who reigned c. 1010–970 B.C.E., is described in the Bible as a skillful harpist, poet, and singer.

**Dreidel:**

> The four-sided Ḥanukkah top with a built-in peg on its bottom, on which it is spun.

**Eighty-five verses:**

> Referring to the eighty-five verses of the biblical Book of Ruth, read on Shavu'ot, focusing on the story of Ruth, the wife of Boaz, and ancestor of David, the king of Israel, who reigned from 1010 to 970 B.C.E. ("Landscaping Mankind's Horizons," page 198.)

**Etrog (plural, Etrogim):**

> A citron ceremonially handled during Sukkot to symbolize learning and charity.

**Four biblical chapters:**

> Referring to the four chapters of the biblical Book of Ruth. ("Landscaping Mankind's Horizons," page 198.)

**Four holiday species:**

> Four species (in Hebrew, *Arba'ah minim*) mentioned in the Bible (Leviticus 23:40): *Etrog* (citron), *Lulav* (palm branch), *Hadassim* (three myrtle twigs), and the *Aravot* (two willow branches). ("Common Possession," page 68.)

**"From Samarkand to Kush":**

> Samarkand, a city in what is now Uzbekistan, and Kush, an ancient African kingdom of Nubia. The expression biblically (*"Mei'Hodu ve'ad Kush,"* Book of Esther 1:1) connotes the distance from India to Ethiopia. ("Who Am I?" page 109.)

**Glasnost:**

> "Openness" in Russian.

**"Go your way . . . with a merry heart":**

> Ecclesiastes 9:7. (" Passover Prayer," page 124.)

**"God is in the midst of her . . .":**

> "God is in the midst of her, she shall not be tumbled down; God shall help her, at the approach of morning" (Psalm 46:6.) ("Holiest of All Shrines," page 178.)

**Gregger (plural, Greggers):**

> A Purim noisemaker used by children to drown out Haman's name whenever mentioned during the reading of the Esther Scroll.

**Hadas (plural, Hadassim):**
> The myrtle.

**Haganah:**
> The volunteer civil defense force associated with the Labor Movement (*Histadrut*) during the British Mandate of Palestine (1920–1948), responsible for laying the foundations of *Zahal*—the Israel Defense Forces.

**Haggadah:**
> A book containing the liturgical text for the Passover *Seder*.

**Hakkafot (singular, hakkafah; in Yiddish, Hakkofes):**
> The joyous processions and dancing around the *Bimah*—the Torah reading platform—with the Torah scrolls on Simḥat Torah.

**Ḥallah (plural, Ḥallot):**
> A braided loaf of bread or cake baked for the Sabbath and festivals.

**Hamantashen:**
> Purim three-cornered filled pastries.

**"He who makes Peace in the Highest":**
> From the *Kaddish*. ("In Bonded Blue and White Bloom," page xxix.)

**"Hear, O ye heavens, and give ear, O earth":**
> Isaiah 1:2. (" Passover Prayer," page 124.)

**"Heavier than the sands of the sea":**
> Job 6:3. ("Simplicity of True Justice," page 55.)

**High Holidays:**
> Rosh ha-Shanah and Yom Kippur are also known as "Days of Awe"— *Yamim Noraim* (Hebrew)—extending, according to the Talmud, from Rosh ha-Shanah through Yom Kippur.

**Holocaust:**
> The murder of six million European Jews by the German Nazis during World War II.

**"I have called with my whole heart; answer me, O Lord . . .":**
> Alluding to the spiritual tenor of the Psalm 119:145. ("Kaddish of Whys," page 147.)

**"I–Thou Relationship":**
> A basic principle of Martin Buber's philosophy whereby the individual maintains an ongoing dialogue with the Creator.

**"If I am I because I am I":**
> See "Sage of Kotzk."

**"If I forget You, O Jerusalem":**
> Psalm 137:5 ("Higher Than Dreams," page 175.)

**"In the courts . . .":**
> "In the courts of the Lord's house, In the midst of thee, O Jerusalem. Hallelujah" (Psalm 116:19). ("Burning Bush," page 195.)

**"Inside an enigma":**
> "A riddle wrapped in a paradox inside an enigma"—a Winston Churchill characterization of the Soviet Union. ("Troika," page 188.)

**Jeremiah's sparkling light—to *seek* You and to *find* You:**
> Alluding to the passage, "And ye shall seek Me, and find Me, when ye shall search for Me with all your heart" (Jeremiah 29:13). ("Heavenly Microchips," page xxviii.)

**Jewish Queen:**
> Queen Esther, the wife of Ahasuerus, King of Persia (Xerxes I), whose story is told in the biblical Book of Esther. It is one of the five scrolls in the Hagiographa section of the Bible. The story, while imbued with religious fervor and dependence on providential rescue, does not mention God's name at all in its narrative (comparable in this respect to Song of Songs [Canticles and the Song of Solomon]). *Megillat Esther*—the Book of Esther, in Hebrew—is the source of the colorful liturgical text for Purim.

**Kaddish:**
> The mourner's Aramaic prayer recited standing. In it the departed is not mentioned. *Kaddish* is a Hymn of Praise relating to an Ezekiel 38:23 prophecy and beginning with the words: "Magnified and sanctified be Your great Name throughout the world. . . ."

**Kavvanah:**
> Spiritual devotion, absolute concentration, outright intention, wholehearted meditation.

**Kinot:**
> Mourning verse, in this context meaning the Book of Lamentations, which is read on the night of Tisha be-Av (ninth day of the month of *Av*).

**Klal Yisrael:**
> The Jewish People; all Jews.

**Kleine menschelech:**
> Literally, "small people" (Yiddish); the ordinary people; the common folk. Used by Shalom Aleichem as the title of one of his books.

**"A lamp unto my feet"** :
> Alludes to the biblical verse: "Thy word is a lamp unto my feet" (Psalm) 119:105). ("A Lamp Unto My Feet," page 10.)

**Latkes:**
> The Ḥanukkah potato pancakes.

**Levi Yitzḥak ben Sarah of Berdichev (c. 1740–1810):**
> Rabbi Levi Yitzḥak's teachings had a profound impact beyond his own generation. In his classic *Kaddish* entitled *"A din Toyre mit Got"* (in Yiddish—a Torah lawsuit with God), he expresses on behalf of the Jewish people his love for the Creator and, simultaneously, a reverent rebuke for His lapses of judgment. Levi Yitzḥah—the founder of Hasidism in Poland— widely known as "ben Meir" (the son of Meir—his father's name, as customary in the traditional Hebrew form of the name), introduced himself in his *Kaddish* as "ben Sarah"—the son of Sarah.

**Lulav (plural, Lulavim):**
> During Sukkot, a bundle consisting of a long palm branch twined with myrtle and willow twigs, symbolizing the season of gladness and waved ceremonially with the *etrog* during the chanting of the *Hallel ha-Gadol* (Psalms 113–136).

**"Masses yearning to breathe free":**
> Emma Lazarus's famed line from her poem "The New Colossus," inscribed on the pediment of the Statue of Liberty. ("Dispatch," page 135.)

**"May the Lord bless you from Zion . . .":**
> Psalm 128:5. ("You'll Never Despair," page 4.)

**"May we unite":**
> Alluding to the collective tenor of the prayer liturgy. ("Entwined Blood Vessels," page 8.)

**Megillah:**
> A scroll containing the Book of Esther.

**Mezuzah (plural, Mezuzot):**
> A rolled parchment scroll inscribed with Deuteronomy passages (6:4–9 and 11:13–21) inserted in a small tube or box of wood, metal, glass, or ceramic, and affixed to doorposts of Jewish homes, schools, synagogues, and so on. According to ancient custom, those leaving or entering the dwelling are required to touch the *mezuzah* with their fingertips, which in turn are brought to their lips and kissed.

**Midrashic:**
> A broad term related to the discussion of nonliteral meanings of language, especially in the Bible, and contained in the Midrash, written in the first century C.E.

**"Millennial Light":**
> Inspired by the aphorism: "We light one candle from another—one is lit, the other is not diminished," from *Midrash* (*ba-Midbar Rabbah* 13). ("Ḥanukkah Portals," page 94.)

**Miracle of Miracles:**
> The Hasmonean miracle of the few prevailing over the many, not by might, but by spirit. ("Ḥanukkah Portals," page 94.)

**Mishnah** (plural, **Mishnayot,** also **Mishnayos**):
> A magisterial compendium of oral laws compiled and codified by Judah ha-Nasi (about 200 B.C.E.) included in the Talmud.

**Mo'adim le-Simḥah!:**
> A Hebrew holiday greeting: Happy Holidays! (literally: Holy Days for Rejoicing). ("Passover Prayer," page 124.)

**Moses, "whom the Lord knew face to face":**
> "And there arose not a prophet since in Israel like Moses, whom the Lord knew face to face" (Deuteronomy 34:10). ("Poetry of the Universe," page 158.)

**"Murdered poets":**
> Twenty-four leading Jewish poets and writers were murdered in the KGB's Lubyanka prison (now a museum), Dzerzhinsky Square, Moscow, on the night of August 12, 1952. According to the poetess Lina Shtern, who was at that time sentenced to life imprisonment (released and died later that year), the last words of David Bergelson, one of the 24 massacred poets, were, "Earth, O Earth, do not cover my blood." ("Beware of Truth," page 185.)

**Naglost:**
> A Russian word meaning lawless insolence and referring to the post-Soviet corruption.

**"Never-failing stream":**
> Paraphrasing Amos 5:24, "Let justice roll down as waters, and true justice as a never failing stream." ("Landscaping Mankind's Horizons," page 198.)

**"Next year in Jerusalem":**
> A blessing from the Passover *Haggadah*, expressing the millennial yearning of the Jews for Jerusalem. ("Aptitude for Liberty," page 121.)

**Niggun** (plural, **Niggunim**):
> A melody, vocal or instrumental, liturgical or entertaining; Jewish soul music.

**Nine candles:**

> The "nine" comprise the eight Ḥanukkah candles with the additional one—"*shammash*" (the server), which is first lit and then used to kindle the others. (Ḥanukkah Portals," page 94.)

**"Nine-tenths of the world's beauty":**

> Inspired by the talmudic idea, "Ten measures of beauty were given to the world, nine were given to Jerusalem, and one to the rest" (Talmud, *Kiddushin*). ("Earthly Custodian," page 176.)

**"Open the blind eyes, to bring out the prisoners from the dungeon, and them that sit in darkness out of the prison-house":**

> Isaiah 42:7. ("Simplicity of True Justice," page 55.)

**Palmaḥ:**

> Commando-like field units (*P'lugot Maḥatz*) of *Haganah*, the underground civil defense forces of prestate Israel during the British Mandate of Palestine (1920–1948).

**Pamyat:**

> An ultranationalistic Russian movement, founded in 1980, still active and growing in Ukraine and Russia. It was technically illegal in the former Soviet Union; under Gorbachev's reform, it was tolerated in spite of its surge of virulent anti-Semitism under the pretext of *glasnost*'s freedom of speech.

**Perestroika:**

> "The act of restructuring" in Russian.

**Perfect the Universe—Tikkun Olam:**

> "To perfect the universe in the Kingdom of the Lord." From *Aleinu* ("It is incumbent upon us [to praise the Lord of all things]"), a concluding prayer of Jewish liturgy. ("Tomorrow Is Too Late," page 208.)

**Persian king:**

> King Ahasuerus (Xerxes I), a king of ancient Persia, husband of the biblical Queen Esther. ("Who Am I?" page 109.)

**Pithom and Raamses:**

> Store-cities built by the ancient Israelites for the Pharaoh, mentioned in Exodus 1:11.

**Plague:**

> The plague that, according to the Talmud (*Yevamot* 62b), killed 24,000 disciples of Rabbi Akiva. ("Hundred-Generation Saga," page 167.)

**"Pliant as a reed and not hard as cedar":**

> An old saying counseling the need for self-protective strength, yet always balanced by humane self-restraint. *Mishnah Ta'anit* 20b. ("Courage of Compromise," page 92.)

**"Precepts of the Lord are right and rejoice the heart":**
> Psalm 19:9. ("Common Possession," page 68.)

**Prophet's Oracle:**
> In the context of Eighteen Gates, the term relates to prophetical warnings related but not limited to Jeremiah's sermons, lamentations, and oracles of judgment. ("Trial of Seismic Gravity," page 53.)

**Rabbi Simeon bar Yoḥai:**
> A prodigious sage and miracle worker; a freedom fighter against Roman rule in the second century C.E.; regarded as one of the principal authors of the Book of *Zohar* (a kabbalistic work), whose day of death, according to the tradition, is commemorated on the 33rd day of *Sefirat ha-Omer* (the Counting of the Omer).

**Refusenik:**
> A term, usually associated with the Jewish human rights movement in the former U.S.S.R: a Soviet Jew denied permission to emigrate from the Soviet Union.

**Sabra:**
> The Mediterranean prickly-pear cactus; in colloquial modern Hebrew, a person born in Israel, thorny and tough on the outside, but inside tender and sweet.

**Sage of Kotzk** (also known as **Der Kotsker,** or **Menaḥem Mendel of Kotsk**):
> Rabbi Mendel Morgenstern (1787–1859), a talmudic scholar and a beloved hasidic leader, is remembered for his epigrammatic interpretation of the well-known Hillel the Sage (first century B.C.E.) saying, " If I am only for myself, what am I?" with the thought-provoking *"If I am I because I am I, and you are you because you are you, then I am I and you are you."*

**"Saving a single life is saving every living thing":**
> A paraphrase of "Whoever causes the loss of a single soul is as though he caused the loss of a world entire, and whoever saves one is as though he saved a universe" (Talmud, *Sanhedrin*). ("Partners for Life," page 62.)

**"Seal us in the Ledger of Life":**
> From *Neilah*—a prayer of the Concluding Sevice on the Day of Atonement. ("Impending Verdict," page 54.)

**Seder:**
> A Passover ceremonial meal commemorating the Exodus from Egypt (1860–65 B.C.E.).

**Set it above your chiefest joy . . .:**
> Paraphrasing "If I set not Jerusalem above my chiefest joy" (Psalm 137:5). ("Friendship," page xxxv.)

**Seven bounties of Eretz Yisrael (in Hebrew, *shiv'at ha-minim*—seven species):**
Crops mentioned in Deuteronomy 8:8 referring to the Land of Israel as "a land of wheat and barley, and vines and fig-trees and pomegranates, a land of olive-trees and honey." ("Common Possession," page 68.)

**Seven-Year Rhythm:**
Referring to "the seventh year thou shalt let it rest" (Exodus 23:10). A biblical ecological-agricultural injunction to let fields lie fallow every seventh year. ("Scripts and Postscripts," page 29.)

**Seventh Month:**
Rosh ha-Shanah falls in the seventh month of the Jewish calendar—*Tishri*. (The first month of the Jewish calendar is *Nisan*.) ("New Beginning," page 43.)

**"Seventy Faces of the . . . Holy Torah":**
According to Jewish mysticism, the Torah has been blessed with seventy faces—mentioned in the Book of Splendor (*Zohar* 1:47). ("Seventy Faces of the Torah," page 37.)

**Shabbat ha-Malkah—(in English, The Sabbath Queen):**
The Sabbath Day—the day of joy, peacefulness, and spiritual harmony—is lovingly referred to as the *Sabbath Queen* and as the *Sabbath Bride*. It is welcomed by kindling at least two Sabbath lights (in some families one candle is kindled for each member). The mistress of the house is traditionally entrusted with the duty of lighting the Sabbath candles.

**Shabbat Shalom:**
A Sabbath greeting in Hebrew (literally, "Sabbath peace!").

**Shalom Aleichem:**
A Sabbath greeting (in Hebrew) meaning "Peace be with you." It is also a Friday Night's *zemirot* hymn sung during the Sabbath meal.

**Shofar (plural, Shofarot):**
A ram's horn is sounded on Rosh ha-Shanah—"a day of sounding *Shofar*" (Numbers 29:1–6). Its importance in Jewish piety and thought goes back to Exodus 19:16: "And it came to pass on the third day, when it was morning, that there were thunders and lightnings and a thick cloud upon the mount, and the voice of a *shofar* exceeding loud; and all the people that were in the camp trembled." *Shofar* is mentioned in the Bible no fewer than 72 times.

**Shulḥan Aruḥ:**
Code of Jewish Law codified by Rabbi Joseph Caro(1488–1575) of Safed, published in 1564–1565.

**Six Thousand Souls of Gold:**
"Six thousand" alludes to the six thousand defenders (four thousand soldiers and two thousand civilians) who gave their lives in defense of Israel during its War of Liberation, 1948–1949. ("Six Thousand Souls of Gold," page 161.)

**Solomon, "in whom was the wisdom of God, to do justice":**

Alluding to his wisdom in making the "true motherhood" judgment: "And all Israel heard of the judgment which the King had judged; and they feared the king, for they saw that the wisdom of God was in him, to do justice" (1 Kings 3:28). ("Untouchable Light," page 160.)

**Symphonie Fantastique:**

An orchestral work by Hector Berlioz (1803–1869) of proportions described as "gigantic," meaning, in this context, the grand design of spirit and fantasy of mind.

**Tallit (plural, Talliyot or Tallitot, also Tallitim; Yiddish, Taleisim):**

A tasseled—preferably made of wool—prayer shawl with fringes stitched with multiples of four threads attached on its four wings (corners) (Numbers 13:58—Commandment of Fringes) worn at every Morning Service and each *Musaf* (Additional Service). On Tish'ah be-Av it is worn for the Afternoon Service instead of for the Morning Service. On Yom Kippur the *tallit* is worn for all five Day of Atonement services.

**Tefillin:**

Phylacteries—two small, ritual, leather cubes bound with straps to the left arm and head during the weekday Morning Service (the afternoon service on Tish'ah be-Av) and containing four biblical inscriptions: Exodus 13:1–10; 11–16; Deuteronomy 6:4–9; 13–21.

**"This Day for Israel":**

"This day for Israel is light and gladness—Sabbath of contentment": one of the most beloved hymns from the *zemirot* for Friday Night ("Day of Calm and Peace," page 30.)

**Tikkun Olam:**

A mystical process of perfecting (putting to rights) the universe through adherence to faith and purity of life that was promulgated by Rabbi Isaac Luria of Safed (1534–1572), known also as the *Ari*.

**The Time of Singing Is Come:**

From Song of Songs 2:12. (page viii.)

**Tish'ah be-Av:**

The Ninth of *Av*, a Day of Mourning.

**Titus's Arch:**

A triumphal arch in Rome, erected by the Romans to commemorate Titus's victory in 70 C.E., and thus indicating Rome's pride in being able to quell Jewish revolt against the Empire.

**"Tree of Life":**

"The Torah is a tree of life to those who cling to it" (Proverbs 3:18). ("Growing with the Trees," page 101.)

**"Troika":**

> A group of three of anything, specifically the Russian three-horse team that pulls a sleigh or carriage.

**"Tummling":**

> Performing prankishly; physical and mental somersaults. A term referring to Catskill Mountains Jewish comedians. Richard F. Shepard, in *Live and Be Well* (Richard E. Shephard and Vicki Gold Levi, Ballantine Books, New York, 1982), captions a photograph of Danny Kaye in a clownish pose as "*still tummling*" and lists Moss Hart and George S. Cohen among *tummlers*. *Tummling* is related to the word *tumult*, and to the Yiddish/German word *tümmlen*—to make noise, to be boisterous.

**Tzedakah:**

> Meaning, in Hebrew, *charity*, and related in the broader biblical and Hebrew language concept to *justice*.

**Ve-im'ru: Amen.**

> Now respond: Amen. ("In Appreciation, " page ix; "Wavelengths of Destiny," page xxx.)

**Wall:**

> See "Western Wall," below.

**"Wannsee Protokoll":**

> The *Wannsee Conference*'s minutes, recorded by Adolf Eichmann, on January 20, 1942, at the Wannsee villa in Berlin (now serving as the Germany's first memorial to the Jews who were murdered by the Nazis). The Wannsee Protocol formalized the guidelines for implementing Hitler's *Endlösung der Judenfrage (*Final Solution*), gruesomely detailing the plans and techniques for the destruction of European Jews.

**"Watchman, what of the night? The watchman said: 'The morning cometh and also the night' ":**

> Isaiah 21:11. ("Ascending Light," page 89; "Six Thousand Souls of Gold," page 161.)

**"We are our beloved's and our beloved is ours":**

> Alluding to Song of Songs 2:16, paraphrased: "Our beloved is ours, and we are hers." ("The Queen," page 26.)

**Western Wall:**

> The holiest shrine of Judaism: the Western Wall of Jerusalem, the last remnant (195 feet in length) of Herod's reconstruction of the Second Temple compound of Jerusalem, destroyed by the Romans in 70 C.E.

**Whale:**

> Allegorically referring to the biblical story of Jonah, the prophet, who was rescued by "a large fish" (Jonah 2:1–11).

**Wheat and barley, vines and fig-trees, and pomegranates; land of olive-trees and honey:**

> A reference to the seven biblical kinds of edible products (Deuteronomy 8:8). ("Common Possession," page 68.)

**"Wholeness of broken dreams":**

> In the spirit of the maxim of Rabbi Mendel Morgenstern (Mendel of Kotzk): "There's nothing as whole as a broken heart." ("Kaddish of Whys," page 145.)

**"Wickedness":**

> "And God saw that the wickedness of men was great in the earth" (Genesis 6:5). ("Kaddish of Whys," page 147.)

**"Woman of Valor":**

> Proverbs 31:10.

**Yad:**

> In Hebrew (literally, "hand" [with a pointing finger]). The hand-shaped pointer is used to indicate to the reader's eye the portion to be read from the Torah scroll.

**Yiddishkeit:**

> Though meaning "Jewishness" in Yiddish, in the context of this book it implies a broad spiritual connotation, embracing Ashkenazic, Sephardic, Yemenite, and Ethiopian traditions, and other related expressions of Jewish communal, cultural, and spiritual life. Shalom Aleichem describes *Yiddishkeit* as "the entire complex of Judaism"; Y. L. Peretz simply says: "*Yiddishkeit* is the Jewish way of looking at things."

**"Yitgadal ve'yitkadash . . .":**

> First line of the *Kaddish*, related to an Ezekiel 38:23 prophecy: "Thus will I magnify Myself, and sanctify Myself, and I will make Myself known in the eyes of many nations; and they shall know that I am the Lord." ("Kaddish of Whys," page 145.)

**Yom Tov:**

> Holiday (noun), in this context means "festive" (adjective); in Hebrew, literally, "Good Day."

**"Zeal for the Lord . . .":**

> 1 Kings 19:20. ("Elijah's Cup," page 140.)

**Zemirot:**

> Sabbath table hymns and poems sung during *Seudah Shelishit* (Third Meal) in the Hasidic-Ashkenazic tradition. In the Sephardic and Yemenite traditions *piyyutim* refers to psalms, *zemirot*, and other scriptural verses of thanksgiving.

# Alphabetical Index
# Holiday Greetings, Meditations, Poems, and Prayers

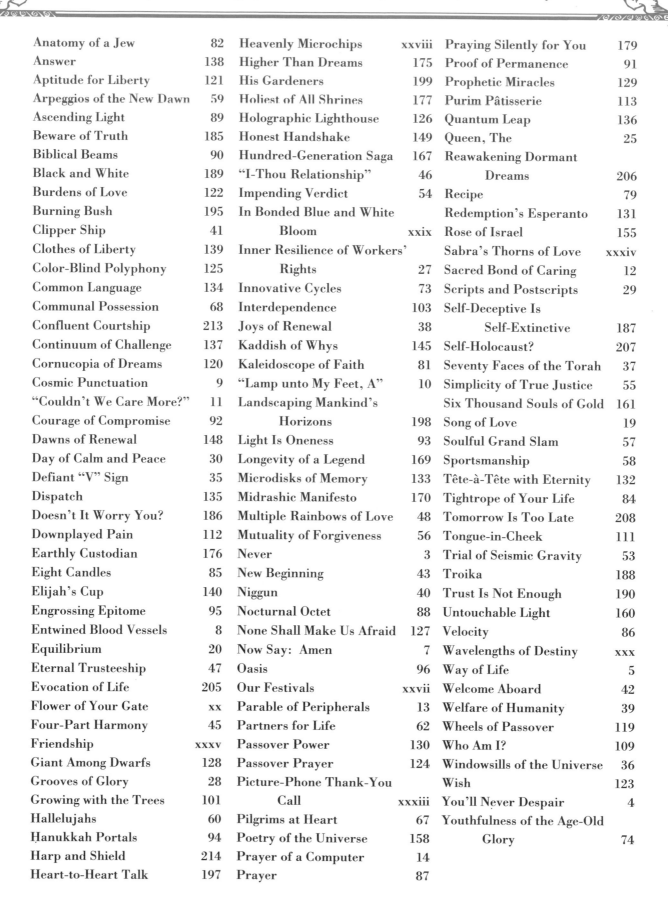